100

WAYS TO START SMART
and get ahead in your career

ELIZABETH J. CLARK
ELIZABETH F. HOFFLER

S2C2 PUBLISHING

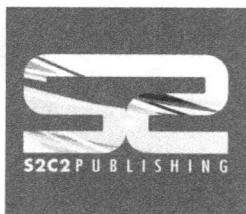

StartSmartCareerCenter.org

100 WAYS TO START SMART
AND GET AHEAD IN YOUR CAREER

Cover design and layout by Martha Rothblum

Printed in the USA

ISBN: 978-0-9908826-0-2
Library of Congress Control Number: 2014922697

CONTENTS

Section 4. Valuable Skills

Section 5. Office Etiquette

Section 6. Office Politics

Section 7. Character Cultivation

Section 8. Boss Management

Section 9. Life Matters

Section 10. Food For Thought

INTRODUCTION

ELIZABETH J. CLARK

Women who entered the workforce during the 1970s and 1980s did not have as many choices as young women today. Some graduate programs and some occupations were almost closed to women. Each of us from that era has memories of fighting sexism and inequality in the workplace.

I can recall a professor who told me I "worked under too many handicaps" to get a doctorate. When I asked what they were, he noted that I was married and had children. Another time I was offered a lower starting salary than advertised. When I questioned the amount, the administrator replied, "Well, aren't you married?" implying that my husband's salary would more than compensate for my loss of income.

These examples seem laughable—and perhaps even illegal— now, but not all of the workplace battles for women have been won. Sexism is alive and well in many organizations. Women still earn 77 cents for every dollar a man makes in the same job. When multiplied out over a career, this difference is staggering and has significant implications for retirement and standard of living.

Additionally, while women now earn more college and graduate degrees than their male counterparts, we have yet to permanently crack and dismantle the glass ceiling. We applaud the progress that has been made while recognizing that only 20 of 100 Senators are women, and women hold only 4.6 percent of CEO positions in Fortune 500 companies. There is still much work to be done for equality for women in the power structure.

One of the advantages of being part of the "Women's Movement" has been the great support and advice women provided for each other along the way. We needed to stick together to make an impact. Most women of my generation did not succumb to the "Queen Bee Syndrome" where, if they reached the top, they tried to keep other women down. Instead, we realized that helping one woman get ahead was a success for all of us.

If we were very lucky in our careers, we had one or two or more outstanding mentors who helped us along the way. They were our graduate thesis advisors, our internship and lab supervisors, our hiring managers, our coaches, and our role models. They supported us and taught us what we needed to know to move forward. Each of us who had a woman like that in our corner owes an enormous debt of gratitude to professional women everywhere.

This compilation of career tips is designed for the woman just beginning her professional journey. It was co-written by two of us, one nearing the end of a long and rewarding career and one a millennial in the first decade of her professional life. We have worked together and have been co-thinkers for eight years. From that partnership, we have identified 100 topics we believe young women need to know to start smart and to get ahead in their careers.

ELIZABETH F. HOFFLER

Women and girls have, indeed, made great strides in all areas of American society. Women can decide for themselves if they want to "lean into" the workplace or raise a family fulltime. Women live longer than men, have higher graduation rates at all levels, and evidence shows that women often have an advantage when it comes to their particular leadership skill set. Yet, when women do fall behind men, it has become known as an "ambition gap" rather than a complex confluence of factors which still affect women in profound ways.

Issues like an increased minimum wage, a strong healthcare system and social safety net, adequate child care options, and the availability of quality education programs are all disproportionality women's issues. However, the world, in terms of resources, policies, and opportunities, was built by, and for, men and we continue to feel the repercussions of a system that was intended to cater to only 50 percent of the population.

It is naïve to assume that our work is done. Every woman I know has stories about being stereotyped, belittled, discriminated against, harassed, ignored, or treated poorly in some way. Women can exhibit the same behaviors as men and be perceived completely differently. Instead of being seen as assertive, we are strident. Yet, if a woman does not exhibit clear strength, any perceived weakness is exploited. If you are too good at your job, you might be seen as competition. If a hint of emotion is shown, it's blamed on hormones.

The data, anecdotes, and stories found in this book should frustrate any woman. The good news, however, is that the women who came before us overcame incredible obstacles and persevered so that we could enjoy unprecedented rights and opportunities today. How will we choose to build on their struggles? Will we take their efforts for granted or will we honor them and support one another as we progress through our careers? Women have a certain responsibility (both to ourselves and to each other) to continue this fight, in all areas of our lives, and push to create a world that is actually equitable.

Those of us who have been fortunate to have strong female mentors in our lives, undoubtedly, have an incredible advantage. Without someone to turn to during your formative career years, the workplace can be an intimidating place that threatens to swallow those who don't figure out how to navigate it. When you do have someone in your corner—a woman who has your best interests at heart, who will be honest with you (in good times and bad), and who will push you to accomplishments that you never would have considered—it is arguably the most important step you can take to reach your professional goals. We know that not everyone finds such a mentor, which is why we've compiled this book of career advice. Written from the perspective of both a mentor and mentee, we think that every woman has the right to start smart and fulfill her potential.

IMAGE MANAGEMENT

Mind Your Mentoring

When you land your first "real" job, it's an exciting time. You finally get to put to use all of the knowledge and skills that you gathered throughout your education. All of the time, energy, and money that you committed to becoming a professional will finally pay off. You will probably feel like there is nothing that you can't handle.

However, it can also be a challenging time. When you begin your career, you inevitably will be faced with colleagues and situations that will test you in new ways. There is no amount of education that can prepare you for these moments. Office politics, unspoken seniority and hierarchy rules, and colleagues' quirks will all present you with unique predicaments. You will accidentally upset people, get stuck in the middle of disputes, and make wrong decisions. It will be much more difficult to navigate these situations without some help. The single most important thing you can do is find a mentor.

Your mentor might be your boss, a close colleague, a professor, or someone within your profession. This person should have a lot in common with you, so that your relationship is comfortable and enjoyable. They also need to be separate enough from you so that competition is not a concern. They should commit to your personal growth and be dependable. There is a mutual respect in a successful mentorship relationship. They need to be honest and objective enough to give you real feedback that could be hard for friends and family to deliver. They should also have significant experience so that they can guide you when you hit road bumps in your career, because they, too, have dealt with these setbacks, and have gotten through them. They can help you understand what is important and what is not.

There are times when we all question ourselves. As women, we must have a support system—other women who can gently correct us when we're wrong, and build us back up when we think we've really screwed up. They celebrate our accomplishments. They encourage us to take the next step in our careers. When you find the right mentor, you will not want to let them down. That is an incredible gift to give yourself, especially early in your career.

Be Your Own Career Coach

Mentors and exceptional bosses are important to guide young professionals. However, not everyone has the luxury of having help at every step of her career. During those times when guidance is missing, it's important to view yourself as your own career coach. Use all of the resources at your disposal and be as informed as you can possibly be when you have to make judgments. Take your time and be methodical in your decisions. Think about the behavior and actions of women you admire. Ask yourself what they would do in your situation. Reach out to them. More often than not, they will be happy to answer your professional questions.

Don't shy away from new challenges. If you need to write a grant proposal, there are plenty of examples for you to review. If you are supervising employees for the first time, advocate for yourself so that your employer will send you to a management course. You might be asked to plan an event. Search online for checklists and resources to help guide you. If you have to give a presentation, even just for your coworkers, take the opportunity to be well prepared and impress everyone with your skills and knowledge.

You also need to look to the future. If you want a certain position that requires a higher degree, figure out what you need to do to earn it. If you think you'd like to move into another department or position at your job, figure out what steps you need to take to make that move. If your dream job is with another organization, determine the best game plan to get there.

Your formal education was just the beginning of building your professional toolkit. Learn as much as you can. Stay up to date on industry standards, technology, and emerging issues. Network with similar professionals. Read industry literature and online publications that can help you gain new perspectives.

Never stop moving towards your goals, and always have new goals to challenge yourself and stay engaged in your work.

Brand Yourself

You will spend your entire career building your reputation—or what is now known as your "personal brand." People in your industry will learn what to expect from you based on what you portray to the world and a range of experiences that they have with you. Every email you send, meeting you facilitate, outfit you wear, comment you make, promise you follow up on, paper you write, presentation you give, and decision you choose build your personal brand.

With the advent of social media tools, your personal brand is now expanded to everyone who has the least bit of curiosity about you. Your personal and professional activities are tracked online, and you become a composite of each picture, video, tweet, message, memo, and post that you leave online. Your personality is broadcast to the world. Even not having an online presence gives an indication of what your brand is.

Keep this in mind when you interact, whether in real life or on the internet. Building a positive brand takes time, energy, and careful planning. It also doesn't take many mistakes to destroy all of your hard work. Think about what you want your brand to be and carefully curate what you portray to the world.

Curb Your Enthusiasm, Pollyanna

Many of us have heard about Pollyanna, the little girl who always saw a silver lining for every situation, who always found something to be glad about even in dire situations. Today, the word itself is used to refer to a person who is unusually upbeat and optimistic, perhaps overly so. There is even a concept in psychology literature, called the "Pollyanna Principle" where people tend to have a bias in remembering things in the past as more positive than they actually were.

Being positive is a welcome trait in most work environments. Blind optimism and naïveté, which often tend toward denial, are not. You may personally believe that something good comes out of every situation, but your coworkers or boss might not see it that way when the team has missed its annual revenue goal or when the grant was just awarded to another organization. Trying to point out the positives in such situations may make you appear unrealistic and immature.

Before you jump in with a favorite cliché or try to cheer people up, do a quick assessment of the moods of your colleagues and your boss. Are they open to input at this point? Is now the best time to put forth your optimistic philosophy? Are they looking for a scapegoat? Will they assume you don't understand the significance of the situation and quickly disregard your suggestions?

It may be a better approach to hold back and look for what can be learned from a setback or missed opportunity. Analyzing what went wrong and discussing future alternatives and actions is a professional and thoughtful response. Timing your remarks is important.

Positivity and enthusiasm have their place. However, unless you temper their expression with the reality of the situation, you will be labeled the office Pollyanna, the little girl who plays "glad games." This image is not what you want to project if you want to be taken seriously.

Learn How to Accept a Compliment

Being recognized for hard work or success is a positive thing for most employees. Yet, it is surprising how few people can graciously accept a compliment.

Receiving personal praise may be a bit uncomfortable, but receiving public accolades can be especially embarrassing. Recipients often squirm or try to deflect the compliment by phrases such as, "It was nothing," or, "I don't deserve the credit." Others try to use humor to mask their discomfort, but that can fall flat and increase the embarrassment.

During your career, you will have many opportunities to accept praise and awards. It's important that you develop ways to deal with this comfortably and professionally. Begin by observing how others handle compliments and make note of responses you admire.

Many times, a simple "thank you," is all that is needed. If "thank you" alone doesn't seem sufficient, you can add another short phrase such as, "This means a lot to me," or, "That's very kind of you."

If you are a candidate for a competitive award, think about possible acceptance remarks ahead of time. You don't want to be unprepared if your name is called. Again, simplicity is often the best approach. Stating that you are grateful for the honor may be sufficient. If you have a person or your team to thank, do so briefly and sincerely. Don't get carried away and read a lengthy list of those who have helped along the way. If you want individuals to know you are grateful for their support and encouragement and that you couldn't have achieved the milestone without them, send them a personal note expressing your feelings of gratitude. This is more meaningful than briefly mentioning them in a list read from the podium.

If you have been informed in advance that you are going to be honored with an award, ask if there will be time for making short remarks. If you are given one to two minutes, practice your comments in advance to make certain you stay within the allotted time frame. Having someone drone on during an awards ceremony becomes tedious and self-indulgent.

With awareness and practice, you can become more comfortable with compliments and the acknowledgment of your successes. Eventually, you will develop your own style of responding in a way that makes you appear gracious as well as outstanding.

Mea Culpa

Too often women start comments or conversation with something along the lines of, "I'm sorry, but…" or, "This is probably a silly/stupid question…" It is rare to hear a man begin a sentence that way. Women often downplay their expertise and can be hesitant to boldly take a position or make a proclamation. If you preface your comment with a self-deprecating statement, then people are likely to think you are less credible. The definition of apology is "a regretful acknowledgment of offense or failure." If you've neither offended nor failed, save your contrition.

If it's worth saying out loud, chances are you've critically thought about it, and it will be a helpful addition to the conversation. If, on the off chance, you do come across as silly or naïve, accept that and move on. Everyone makes mistakes.

Sometimes you may make a comment that didn't seem to get attention or wasn't accepted very well. After the meeting, however, people may approach you and thank you for speaking up because they were thinking the same thing or appreciated your perspective. As long as you are known for thoughtful, constructive comments, your input will be expected, and more importantly, sought.

Playing Dress Up

We've all heard the old adage, "Dress for the job you want." It's good advice, but, sometimes you are caught in situations that call for a bit more guidance. The best rule of thumb is that if you question, even for a second, what you are wearing, then you should change. This is particularly relevant for women as they determine length of skirt, tightness of fit, height of heel, heaviness of makeup, or strength of perfume.

If you have to ask a coworker if what you're wearing is appropriate, the answer is probably no. Even if you could get by with the outfit in question, your self-esteem will take a hit because you aren't sure of yourself.

It's also wise to look at women you respect for fashion guidance. Women who carry themselves with confidence and demand respect from others will be good role-models in terms of appearance. There will always be differences in terms of age, body type, and personal preference, but it's an easy way to determine what is appropriate for the setting.

The ugly truth, unfortunately, is that we are all judged by our appearance...at least initially. Women are typically judged more harshly than men. Wearing a dress that is going to be perfect for your date after work may mean that you're taken less seriously at your meeting that day. You might be tired after a late night, but the next morning when you wake up late and look sloppy could be the day that you're called into your CEO's office for a report. Your heels could look spectacular, but if you can't walk in them properly, you will look ridiculous.

Every workplace and industry is different, but it's wise to indeed dress for the job you want, at least until you find the balance between what is expected of you and what makes you comfortable. Your appearance can signify how serious you are about your work, so think carefully the next time you open your closet.

Practice What They Preached

As teenagers, most of us probably got tired of advice about common courtesy from our parents and grandparents. How many times were we told to "stand up when you are introduced to someone," or to "stop mumbling," or to "answer when someone asks you a question?" We had our grammar and table manners corrected, and we sometimes wondered if they would really be important later in life.

Good business etiquette is not far removed from the advice given to us in our childhood and adolescence: Always stand up when introduced to someone. Practice shaking hands and get some feedback on your handshake. Make sure you look directly at the person you are meeting. Don't mumble. Don't be overly familiar. Use their title and last name unless invited to call them by their first name. Use appropriate language and good grammar.

Some companies make it a habit to take job applicants to lunch or dinner. This outing helps them gauge your level of comfort and sophistication. They don't want to hire you and then find out you are an embarrassment when you are in a more formal or public setting.

As you start up the career ladder, you may find that you could benefit from taking a short course on business etiquette, especially if you travel to another country where business manners differ or where they take on even greater importance. Deals can be lost because you have inadvertently offended your foreign host.

And, when you get a chance, thank your family for their good advice.

Rant Management

Most employees manage to keep their emotions under control fairly well in the office. At times, there may be some curt responses, sarcasm, or humor at others' expense. Or, there may be some spirited debate over work issues or direction. Rants, however, are never acceptable, and they are especially difficult to recover from in the workplace.

Losing control due to anger serves no one well, least of all the "rantee." If you are someone with a short fuse, you need to have an escape plan before you do damage to your reputation. All of us have our emotional triggers. For some, it may be unfairness or rudeness. For others, being wrongly blamed or accused is a flashpoint.

If you feel you are about to lose your temper, get out of the room. Simply say, "Excuse me," and go to the restroom until you have regained control. Or, if possible, you might leave the building for a brief walk. Do not resort to sending negative emails to coworkers or friends. That sort of reaction will not help you resolve the issue.

If your boss has incited your anger, it becomes more delicate to handle. While it might momentarily make you feel better to tell your boss how wrong (or miserable) she is, you can't win that battle. You will come off as defensive, disrespectful, or insubordinate. Sometimes your comments or tone can lead you down a path of no return, and being fired because of your own bad behavior is hard to overcome when looking for a new job.

You know yourself well enough to recognize when your emotions are getting out of control. When you feel that happening, you need time to sort through your feelings and to consider why the situation has made you so angry. When you have calmed down, you will be at a more stable emotional place and your problem solving skills can take over.

Waterworks In the Workplace

Controlling tears is mostly a learned behavior. Both sexes have the genetic ability to shed tears, yet very early on, boys are expected to control theirs while girls are given the message that tears are acceptable in many situations. These situations include when you are hurt (physically or emotionally), when you are exasperated, when you are angry, when you are happy, or when you are sad. We are even told that tears are therapeutic and that "having a good cry" is the answer to handling our feelings.

When a woman enters the workforce, her previous crying behavior must be assessed and probably unlearned. The rule is straight forward—there is no place for tears in the workplace. There may be a few exceptions to this rule like receiving sudden tragic news—but for all other causes, tears must be kept at bay, or at least kept private.

Some may argue that tears can be one way to feminize (read humanize) the workplace, but both male and female colleagues often don't know what to do when someone cries. Crying makes most people feel uncomfortable and inadequate, and crying makes the crier appear unprofessional, even unstable.

So, leave the room, or leave the building if you have to cry. Close your door until you get your emotions and yourself under control. An old commercial used to admonish, "Don't ever let them see you sweat" …or cry.

ATTITUDES FOR SUCCESS

Attention!

We have turned into a multitasking society, and we seem to be proud of that fact. People talk on their smartphones in the grocery aisles, check facts for a report while sitting in traffic, send tweets from various events, and take pictures to post on Facebook at every turn. We are like consumer reporters on 24-hour duty.

At work, multitasking escalates. We participate on a conference call while surfing the web on our laptops. Since we can now work from anywhere on our devices, we are no longer tethered to our desks or to our workspace. We begin one task, get interrupted, and go back to another task that was started and interrupted previously—before the current interruption. There are days when you are too busy being busy to get any real work done. Therein lies the trap of doing too much at once.

The major problem with multitasking is that we only have 100 percent of our attention. We can divide our attention any way we want, but it will still add up to only 100 percent. Multitasking doesn't amplify our capacity to pay attention. In fact, multitasking often decreases our efficiency because it fractures our focus.

At work, consider working sequentially, finishing task A before starting task B. Give your attention to one responsibility at a time or follow your to-do list. It will require some discipline but the rewards will show up in your productivity.

Be Curious

Be curious. Seek knowledge. Read everything you can get your hands on—newspapers, magazines, novels, memoirs, websites, blogs, tweets, and Facebook posts. Read for pleasure and read for business. You should be up to date on the news in your industry, the content area of your organization, and the laws and regulations affecting your work. Offer to proofread documents at work. Ask others to proofread your work. Ask people what their favorite books are. Write down quotes that resonate with you. Read articles from both sides of the aisle. Even keep an eye on the sports section. You never know when it might come in handy during conversation.

This curiosity will enrich your personal and professional lives. It will increase your value at cocktail parties and improve your writing. You will become a more eloquent public speaker and a more engaging conversationalist. You won't feel left out when people are discussing current events and you will be looked to as a resource and an asset.

Your curiosity is a multipurpose tool—keep it sharp and use it often.

Done Is Better Than Perfect

Sometimes our to-do list seems unmanageable. We begin each morning by reviewing what we must accomplish that day. When we check again in the evening, the list isn't shorter; in fact, it has grown. Essential tasks remain unfinished. Other items linger partially completed.

There never seems to be enough time to get through the list. You wonder how your colleagues are keeping up while you are getting further behind. You know you are as smart as they are and you work hard—harder than many of them seem to be working. What do they know that you don't?

Could it be that you are sabotaging yourself? Maybe your list can't get done because of a tendency toward perfectionism. You pride yourself on high standards. You want to do an outstanding job. You remember the advice of your grandmother who always said, "If a job is worth doing, it's worth doing well." If this paragraph describes you, your perfectionism can be leading you to procrastination.

Take a critical look at your list. Recognize that not all tasks require—or deserve—the same amount of time and effort. Identify those items for which good is actually good enough and mark them as such. Get rid of these items as quickly as possible so you can focus on the important issues, on the undertakings that really matter to your boss, or your organization, or your personal life. Strive for progress, not perfection.

Others don't always recognize—or even care about—perfect grammar, perfect structure, or perfect reports. What they do care about is getting the job done. So keep your perfectionism in check and check off your to-do list instead.

Don't Settle For the Cheap Seats

There is going to be a meeting with the boss that will be held in the conference room. Unfortunately, the conference table isn't large enough for all the managers to sit at the table. There are chairs placed around the perimeter of the room for overflow.

The men wander in and take a seat at the table without giving it a second thought. They may try to decide where the boss will sit so they can choose their chair strategically. Some of the women seem uncertain about where to sit and graciously gravitate to the overflow seats. Soon there is a gender divide in the room—men at the table, women on the fringe. Seeing all the seats at the table have been taken, the last man to arrive pulls an additional chair up to the table and squeezes in among his male colleagues. He never even considers sitting anywhere else but at the table.

Don't settle for the cheap seats. Does this sound familiar? It is harder to be a part of the discussion from the sidelines. It is also harder to get your boss's ear or attention from a distance.

The next time you are invited to a meeting, arrive a bit early and choose a good seat at the table. Stake your claim to be part of the conversation. Don't worry about where the men will sit. They will be fine.

You worked hard to buy your full price ticket to the workplace, so take your proper seat.

Manage Your Uncertainty

Unless a professional path is fairly defined, such as becoming a physician or a certified public accountant, it may be difficult to see that straight career path you hoped you were on. You may accept one position only to find that you're not sure you like the field you have chosen. Perhaps you thought you would be good at sales, or would like working in a law firm, or would be good at public service, but then find it isn't quite what you expected or hoped. What now? Do you start over or do you stick it out? If you stick it out, for how long?

While these questions and their answers are different for each individual, there are some general guidelines that might be useful for your present job while you are deciding your future. Most importantly, try your best not to compare your job (or your salary or your life) with those of your friends or your acquaintances, especially in terms of what they simply post on social media. Most people tend to overemphasize their happiness, including their job satisfaction.

Similarly, try not to second guess your decisions. You thought you would like, or do well, in your current position when you accepted the job, so give yourself some time to succeed before you decide it was the wrong choice. Keep in mind that it takes time to build experience and competency in a job or field. If you give your job your best effort, you may find that as you become more proficient, you will feel more positive, or your work may be noticed by a boss and you will be given the additional responsibility you want.

It is also important to seek out and take advantage of any opportunities your job offers. If you are invited to attend meetings, training sessions, or conferences, do so. Volunteer for special projects.

Meet new people. Take advantage of any continuing education or certifications available to you. Check to see if your employer will pay for a relevant course each year or pay for you to prepare to sit for a licensing exam.

Also, keep up to date with new developments in your field. Read newsletters, blogs, and journals. Join a relevant professional society or your alumni association. Find a community service project and volunteer.

Be certain not to burn any bridges. Leaving a job well can be just as important as beginning one. Many occupational fields are smaller than you realize, and that boss you dislike now may be the president of your professional association tomorrow.

Most career paths aren't linear. In your work life, you will hold many different jobs, some great, some mediocre. Along the way, you may change direction, refocus, or even start anew. Each of your jobs adds to your experience base. Each employment situation has some opportunity for honing your skills, for increasing your competency. So take every advantage of the job you have now, even as you prepare for your future career journey.

She's So Emotional

It has been well-documented that women typically have greater emotional intelligence than their male counterparts. Emotional intelligence means that women are sensitive to the emotions, moods, and needs of others. They tend to be more empathetic and understanding.

People who are emotionally intelligent can quickly detect if their boss is frustrated, if colleagues are upset, if employees aren't completely focused, and most importantly, they can understand and manage their own emotions. The eight or more hours that people spend at work constitute the majority of their waking time, which means that people will experience a full range of emotions that can contribute to workplace misunderstandings and conflict. Employees that can perceive the moods of others and successfully analyze motivations, build teams, or diffuse tense situations can be extraordinarily helpful at the office.

Of course, this is not true about all women or all men. Some women are callous and some men are sensitive. Although it is an extremely valuable characteristic for anyone to have, emotional intelligence won't carry you through your career if you have nothing else to offer. Likewise, some people are extremely intelligent but continually offend others with their behavior.

Some individuals seem to have been born with this quality, but it can certainly be strengthened in people for whom it doesn't come naturally. Take the time to observe others and find out what makes them tick. Make an effort to form relationships with your colleagues. Be slow to criticize and try to understand where people are coming from. If you remain calm and are consistently a voice of reason, you will provide an invaluable service for your organization.

The Power of Self-Talk

We talk to ourselves all day long. In fact, if you aren't talking to someone else, you are more than likely carrying on a conversation with yourself. Sometimes we are aware of these intrapersonal conversations, but many times we are not.

You may be sitting in a meeting saying to yourself, "This is so boring, I'm not sure I can get through the hour." Or you may admonish yourself and tell yourself to pay attention or to stop looking so bored. You may replay past conversations with others or rehearse conversations to come. You may work on solving a problem or writing a memo. All of this falls under self-talk.

Most of our self-conversations are helpful or neutral. Some, however, are negative and have the potential to make us anxious or ruin our day.

For example, if you get dressed in the morning and feel a bit off or uncomfortable about what you are wearing, you may reinforce that feeling with negative self-talk throughout the day. If you are having a bad hair day, you may tell yourself about it every time you catch a glimpse of yourself in a mirror or window.

The same is true for work efforts or situations. If you keep telling yourself that your project or report isn't very good, you act in a certain way. If you tell yourself that you did a good job, you act in a different way.

Self-talk can empower you or diminish you. It can amplify your positive or negative feelings. It can impact your work and your self-esteem.

Make a habit of being attuned to your self-talk. Only you have the ability to restate it, to change the conversation, to shift your mood or attitude. Self-talk is a powerful tool in both your personal life and professional career. Be conscious of its power and use it with care.

What's Next?

One of the most invaluable skills any employee can have is knowing what to do next. Managing people is challenging and employers value those individuals who have completed their work and have already moved on to the next thing. Most employees can't work in a vacuum or make autonomous decisions, but they should try to anticipate the needs of their boss (and their organization) and take proactive steps to get things done.

It is predictable and acceptable for interns to need clear direction on what to do next. Even early career professionals need a bit of extra guidance. Once you've been working a few years, though, you should consistently show initiative, and your boss should be able to count on you to come up with new ideas and even inspire her, or the team, to take on new challenges.

Smart workers are never bored because they are always coming up with new ideas, projects, and goals. You want to be the go-to person for innovation and energy, not the person who constantly needs a hand to hold.

Workplace Awareness

Part of growing up is becoming more self-aware. Being more self-aware means learning to recognize your weaknesses as well as your strengths. It also means taking a hard look at how others see you and how they react to the messages you give, often unintentionally.

Perhaps you are uncomfortable with small talk. Not joining in conversations can make you appear stand-offish, even arrogant. If you are used to being the center of attention at home or with your friends, you may unwittingly be competing for attention at meetings and in the workplace.

If you hold strong views, you may not be aware of how your comments, tone, and facial expressions are received by colleagues or clients who have differing opinions. Think for a moment of a person in your office who seems sexist. What behaviors and actions have led to that label for your coworker? Is it just a feeling you have, or are there specific examples of sexist behavior or sexist comments? Does he or she know what others think? Would he or she be surprised by the label?

Oftentimes our lack of self-awareness in the workplace centers around the belief in our competence level or what we think we have personally achieved. It is closely linked to our self-importance. If you find yourself thinking you are the most competent person in the room, or the brightest, or the hardest worker, take a moment to step back and analyze that notion. Would others agree or would they rank your performance a bit lower?

Many beginning professionals are disappointed in their first reviews or annual evaluations. If this is true in your case, be open to suggestions about how you can improve your performance. Ask a trusted colleague for an honest assessment and don't be upset if they answer honestly. The more self-aware you are in the workplace, the greater your chances of maturing into the success you envision.

You Can Do It

While the boundaries are changing slowly, there is still an artificial divide between male and female sports, male and female-dominated occupations, and roles in the workplace and at home. For example, most secretarial or administrative jobs are still held by women. In technology, men continue to outnumber women, although women are gaining steadily.

How you decide who does what in your home is up to you and your partner. In the workplace, though, duties may be dictated by job description, by supervisor, or by habit. If you work in a union shop, crossover of responsibilities may be discouraged or even prohibited.

Maybe your office has decided that all professional staff should do their own back-up including researching issues, writing reports, and preparing media materials. If this is the case where you work, you need to become expert in these areas. If you are struggling with any of them, ask an experienced colleague or friend to teach you what you need to know or take a class outside of work.

While you are at it, figure out how to run the office copier, and how to set up and use a conference phone. This may not be your usual responsibility, and you don't want it to be. However, if you are dependent on the office manager to do these things, you are in trouble if he takes a sick day when an important conference call with a client has been scheduled. Or you are trying to get ready for that big meeting in the morning, and the copier jams or runs out of ink. Or the boss asks for a slide to be redone at midnight and you don't know how to make the change.

Self-sufficiency is important. Being able to depend on your own skills and capabilities gives you confidence. Being or acting helpless in the workplace only perpetuates those old boundaries and stereotypes.

PROFESSIONAL PROTOCOLS

Don't Say Anything At All

Thumper (of Bambi fame) was continually advised by his mother, "If you can't say something nice, don't say anything at all." This advice was wise, but probably didn't go far enough in terms of how people interact at work.

It's common sense that you should not say anything negative to colleagues regarding their appearance. Anyone with manners and common sense knows better than to point out a mismatched outfit or a bad haircut. But what about your coworkers who looks like she's been going to the gym or your colleague who has on a particularly smart outfit?

It's a good practice to not make comments, good or bad, on superficial things in the office. If a coworker has lost weight and you think she looks great, consider that it may be due to something beyond her control (like an illness or an eating disorder). Telling someone they look nice in an outfit may make them think that every other day they aren't up to par. It could also cross the line into what is perceived as harassment if you aren't careful. Comments like, "I just can't believe how much weight you've lost," or, "That color really brings out your eyes," can easily be misconstrued. For women, issues like pregnancy and menopause can make this issue particularly salient. Unless you are personally close to someone you work with, the best policy is to think it, not say it.

Email—Fast, Easy, and Incredibly Important

Emails leave a professional trail and are often the best way to communicate yourself to others. They don't have the pressure of public speaking or the awkward silences of a conversation. You can choose how to portray yourself, and every email is an opportunity for you to shine.

Written etiquette requires a proper salutation and concluding "thank you," even for email. If you don't personally know the person you are writing, say "Dear Ms./Dr./Mr. Smith." Do your research to figure out the proper prefix (for example, you refer to someone with a PhD as Dr.), and introduce yourself and the reason you are writing. Try not to use "To Whom it May Concern." Always thank the person for her time and attention. You should also include a meaningful subject in the subject line. It should be concise, but descriptive. Don't ramble in the body of the email, but provide enough information to inform the reader. Offer to chat on the phone if the recipient needs more information.

Even if you do all this, it could be for naught if your email contains grammatical errors, misspellings, or careless mistakes which broadcast that you don't take your work seriously enough to ensure that your emails are professional. Granted, smartphones make these mistakes increasingly common, but if you consistently send poorly written emails, you won't be trusted to write anything more important.

Finally, use emoticons and exclamation points sparingly or not at all. They are meant to signify excitement. They lose that significance when you use five in one email. Also, there is a time and a place for emoticons. Rarely is it appropriate to send electronic happy faces in the workplace. If you are thanking a close coworker for her help, or making a joke, go ahead and send that winky face if you must, but refrain from trying to figure out which emoticon will best communicate your feelings to your boss. When in doubt, keep it simple, and let your well-written emails further reflect your value to the company.

Media Mindfulness

Most large organizations have specific communications departments or a director of communications or public affairs. These employees are responsible for press releases, answering queries from the media, and overseeing electronic communication. Small shops, however, may not have the luxury of assigning all the related duties to one person, so the possibility of making errors or misstatements that go public becomes a concern.

When you begin a new position, take some time to review policy and determine what, if anything, is within your purview with regard to talking to the media, answering organizational emails, or writing blog entries. A good rule of thumb is to never speak on behalf of your organization without being given the explicit authority to do so.

Keep in mind that representatives from the local press may attend some of the same community meetings you do. When speaking publicly, always choose your words carefully and keep your responses professional.

Sometimes it seems flattering to have a press member ask for a quote or ask you to answer a sensitive question. Their intent may not be as flattering as you think, and nothing is ever really off the record. It's best to decline and offer to refer them to your supervisor or communications director.

If while at work, you are called directly by the press or you answer the phone and a reporter is on the other end, always say you will have to call her back. Even if you have the authority to represent the organization, calling the reporter back allows you time to prepare for the call and to get needed information together so you can provide adequate and accurate data. Likewise, never respond to a blog or negative email in haste. Knee-jerk reactions will just make the situation worse, and once it is out there, you can never take it back.

It is also important to keep in mind that any correspondence on your organization's letterhead is considered official communication. Never use corporate letterhead for personal letters or for political purposes such as writing to a legislator about a concern or about a piece of legislation you support. This correspondence can easily be misconstrued as the company position.

As your career unfolds, try to get as much media training as you can. Attend seminars and talk with colleagues who work with the press or in communications departments. The more you know about the media, the more missteps you can avoid.

Mind Your Own Business

There is a fine line between being energetic and helpful and being obnoxious. Your colleagues are all adults. They have managed to conduct their professional lives for many years without you. If something is far outside of your job description, leave it alone. For instance, you don't need to remind your coworkers about meetings, email them weather warnings, or keep them up to date on news.

This behavior may seem well-intentioned, but it is an unwise use of your time and will eventually be annoying to others. It signifies that you don't think people can be trusted to handle their own business. Focus on your own work. If you are setting a high standard, others will naturally follow.

Responsibility Required

Everyone understands family emergencies. You have a fender bender on the way to work or you get a call from the school nurse saying your child is sick and has to be picked up. These crises generally are few and far between, so bosses are likely to be tolerant.

What employers have a harder time with is when you don't have back-up plans. Maybe your child is having some behavioral problems at school and ends up in the nurse's office complaining of an ailment two or three times a week. Or you have an elderly parent who frequently calls with concerns and requests for your immediate attention. Or your partner's car isn't running and he needs to rely on you for transportation which requires you to come in late or leave early for a couple of weeks.

No one is suggesting that you don't take care of a sick child or an elderly parent. If this is a recurring problem, however, you need to have a good plan for handling the situation.

You may not realize how lucky you are to be in a professional job with flexibility and paid vacation or sick time. There are some jobs, even professional ones, that don't provide much leeway. For example, a nurse can't leave her unit unless there is someone there to take over the responsibility for her patients.

Other jobs have zero tolerance for leaving or missing work. The woman on an assembly line in a factory, the teacher in a small nursery school, the school bus driver, the maid in a busy hotel, or the short order cook at the diner has to have back-up plans. Their pay may be docked or they may lose their jobs altogether if they leave unexpectedly or don't show up.

How ironic that women in professional jobs with great options and support don't feel as much of an obligation to prepare for contingencies as their counterparts with fewer alternatives. Having no back-up plan makes you appear professionally irresponsible mainly because you are being irresponsible and unfair to both your colleagues and your workplace.

Security Priority

Today, security is an important issue for all organizations, but where you work and the type of business generally determine how stringent security will be. Security rules range from simply bothersome to onerous. Maybe you only need to swipe a badge to gain entrance to your building. Perhaps you have to change your network password every month. Or, you may need to sign in and out of the building each time you leave or enter.

On the other hand, if your organization deals in patents or trade secrets, or if it collects confidential data about customers, patients, or donors, the security requirements probably will be much stricter. The repercussions for not adhering to required security measures will also be greater.

As an employee, you need to be aware of and follow all security protocols. Take them seriously. Don't try to bypass them or work around them. For example, trying to talk the security guard at the front desk into letting you pass because you have forgotten your badge puts him in a bad position. His job may, in fact, probably does, depend on 100 percent compliance.

Don't ask to use your coworker's badge or to borrow her password because you forgot to change yours on time and you are locked out of the system. Never give out the security code to office doors or to a parking garage for after-hours use or try to make extra copies of office keys so you have an extra in case you lose the original. Don't copy office files to take home unless this is acceptable procedure.

With regard to confidential data and information, access only what you have a legitimate need for and right to know. Nothing may get you fired quicker than looking at someone's personal file and violating their privacy.

If you breech office security in any way, if you lose your badge, key, or company credit card, report it immediately, no matter how embarrassing it may be. Being momentarily embarrassed is much better than being permanently unemployed.

Big Girl Shoes

Everyone is anxious to begin her first professional job, yet many individuals may not be quite prepared for what they find. Work environments vary greatly in structure, in policy, and in practice. Some have rigid rules for attendance, dress codes, and performance. Others are more flexible. It's critical to know what's acceptable at your workplace.

With regard to dress, it's always better to err on the side of professional attire, at least until you learn the norm. This practice may mean giving up favorite outfits, excessive jewelry and casual clothes like jeans and shirts with logos. Nothing is more embarrassing to your boss than to have you attend a meeting looking more like a college student than a new professional.

You may begin your career in a shared office or cube. Take note of how people decorate, whether or not music or headphones are acceptable, and if it is okay to eat lunch at your desk. Check the employee handbook to determine if you can take personal calls or use your computer for personal reasons. Keep in mind that privacy is often unavailable in offices.

Before you start your first day, do your research to be prepared. For example, you need to be on time. Allowing for traffic or other problems, how much time do you need for your commute? Being late to work is noticed. It's not like missing a class. You can't sleep through your alarm, get to the office late, and do your hair and make-up at your desk.

Also, you will need some contingency plans in case you have unexpected events. Do you know how you will get to work if your usual mode of transportation is not working? What happens if your train is stalled, your car breaks down, or your car pool doesn't come? Do you know an alternate parking space if the garage you use is full or closed for some reason? What happens if you forget your security badge?

These questions and items may seem trivial, but they are not trivial in their consequences. To be treated as a professional, you need to be one—starting with your first day on the job. There are simple steps to starting your professional career on the right foot.

It's Not Worth It

Office supplies have changed over the years. No longer is work done mainly with paper and pencil. Files are kept electronically, and every computer has a calculator, dictionary, and address book. The supply closet at your workplace probably contains usual items such as copy paper, pens, and notebooks, as well as higher priced items such as printing cartridges, USB drives, and batteries.

What hasn't changed is the fact that office supplies belong to your employer and are meant to be used only for work activities. Unless you are sanctioned to work from home, they are not meant for stocking your home office. They are not meant for supporting the efforts of your church or a non-profit organization where you volunteer. They are not there to help you complete the required school supply list for your children or relatives.

Supplies cost employers money, and many places have strict inventory controls. What seems insignificant to you might be significant if hundreds of employees are doing the same thing.

It is easy to pick up a box of pens or a few thumb drives or a ream of paper for your home printer. You figure it will never be missed or that no one will know, and besides that, what can it hurt?

The answer is that it can hurt your career. You could be accused of stealing from your employer. You could be dismissed from your job.

Even if you were only reprimanded, consider how embarrassing it would be to have a supervisor or colleague confront you about a missing box of USB drives or a missing printer cartridge. Think how awkward it would be if you were called down to the human resource office or, worse yet, if your boss were notified.

If you worked in a grocery store you wouldn't take a few unpaid items home with you for dinner. If you worked in a department store, you wouldn't take clothing items to wear without paying for them. Taking office supplies from a professional office is no different.

Never put your reputation or your career at risk for a few pens or a ream of paper. It simply isn't worth it.

The Grammar Police

We've all been taught the importance of good grammar. Whether speaking or writing, grammar shouts, and it says a lot about you. As a professional, you use spell check and double check word usage. You are careful about punctuation and transitions. You may ask a coworker or staff member to review an important memo or document, or ask for feedback before a presentation.

Others in your workplace may not be as conscientious. Some of your colleagues, or even your boss, may not be aware of their grammatical errors. What is your role if you notice poor grammar? Do you try to help in a subtle way or do you become the grammar police?

If an employee reports to you or if your name is going to be on a document, you have a vested interest in having it be correct. Helping an employee recognize that she misuses or misspells certain words will help her in the future, but do it in private, not in front of others.

On the other hand, coworkers may want your input about content, but not sentence structure. Before you review a memo, determine what they are asking you to do. If they only want your comments, read it without making grammatical corrections. If reading in hard copy, it helps to read it without a pen in your hand. If reading online, you might gently suggest the colleague put it through spell check.

If your boss is the author or speaker, your application of grammar rules becomes much more sensitive. You might quietly mention to her executive assistant that you have read the memo or slides and you think there is a typo or two. This effort may result in the assistant making the corrections or pointing out errors to her boss. Unless your boss asks specifically for your editing help, there isn't much you can do.

You may be silently correcting someone's grammar in your head, but it is not your role to arrest anyone for bad grammar.

Workplace Oddities

You quickly find on your first job that you will need to learn about new and even odd things. These nuances probably aren't discussed in school and generally aren't the topics of happy hour conversations. They will require that you spend a bit of extra time researching and understanding them.

For instance, if you are involved with board meetings at your organization, you are going to need to understand *Robert's Rules of*

Order, which are the parliamentary authority guidelines for running official meetings. If you are in charge of your own budget, it is wise to know what Generally Acceptable Accounting Principles (or GAAP) and the Form 990 are. It's helpful to understand the difference in tax structures (such as 501(c)3, 501(c)4, or 501(c)6) for nonprofit organizations. If you're working for a foundation, you should understand what an endowment, planned giving, and annual fund mean. If you've never written a request for proposals (or RFP), you will probably need to figure it out. If you intend on lobbying, you should understand the Honest Leadership and Open Government Act (or HLOGA), which governs lobbying activity. If you are working internationally, do you know what it takes to form a non-governmental organization (NGO)?

Every industry, organization, and even department has different terms and procedures that they either follow because they must legally do so, or because that is how business has always been conducted.

Executives, researchers, clinicians, academics, advocates, communications and PR professionals, fundraisers, writers, IT workers, and everyone else that will cross your professional path will have their own way of communicating. Learning strange workplace terms, policies, and procedures will serve you well and give you a distinct advantage.

VALUABLE SKILLS

A Lost Art

If you learn the art of taking good notes, you will be very valuable to your organization. Taking thorough notes that capture almost everything that is said is a task that few are willing to do. Some people just don't think about the importance of notes, while others believe that note taking is beneath them.

Chances are, you may never look at those notes again, but every now and then someone has a question about what was discussed or who was there, and you will have an account of what occurred. If you are the go-to note taker, you become a good resource. Take the initiative to step into this role.

Another secret about note taking is that it keeps you focused in meetings (especially the ones that aren't thrilling), prevents you from looking bored, and will assist you in recalling important information. The benefits of note taking help ensure that you are an asset to your team and company.

Communication Detraction

Some time ago, a communications professional gave a pitch to a high-powered board of directors. Her content and graphics were excellent. She was well-spoken and engaging. All in all, it was an excellent presentation.

The downside came during the question and answer period. Every time a board member asked a question or made a comment, the presenter began her response with an enthusiastic "absolutely." At first, it felt a bit patronizing. Then it seemed condescending. Eventually, it felt like fingernails on a chalkboard. People were practically cringing with each repetition of the word.

At the program's conclusion, people left remembering her irritating response more than her earlier content. She undid a lot of hard work with a careless approach to the question and answer segment.

When tasked with an important presentation, many of us practice our talk, go over our slides and make certain we are within the time parameters allowed. Few take the time to practice the potential Q and A period. What questions and comments are you expecting? What resistance might be forthcoming? Do you have back-up data readily available? Are there colleagues in the audience ready to support you if needed?

Better than guessing about what might occur, have your work colleagues listen to your pitch and ask questions if something isn't clear. Sometimes you—and even your boss—may be too close to the content to see any loopholes, missing information, or incongruences.

After the practice session, ask a trusted colleague if she has any suggestions for making your presentation better. In the opening example above, any friend or colleague would have noticed the repeated use of "absolutely" and would have suggested omitting it from each answer.

Don't let a haphazard response ruin an otherwise excellent presentation. The take-away message should be on your message, not on your mannerisms. Absolutely.

Details Are Not the Devil

No matter what you are working on—a major project, a memo to your boss, or an email to a colleague, triple check your work. One of the most common mistakes people make is not following through with the small details. Are the dates you are referencing correct (the day of the week matches the numerical date)? When you schedule a meeting with people from across the country, which time zone are you using? Is everyone's name spelled right and do you have their preferred credentials correct? Do you have a plan B in case something goes wrong?

Likewise, if you go to your boss with a request, update, or project summary, know every last detail about what you are discussing. "I don't know" is not an acceptable answer. You are the one with the information, and they need to use your knowledge as a shortcut to make a decision. However, sometimes there is a question that you won't know how to answer. If that happens, say that you will get that answer to them within the hour and then deliver on your promise. Recognize the power you have to be the conduit to important information.

Read everything in detail. This task might mean spending time on your train ride home going over materials again, reading memos while you work out, or catching up on work while your roommate or partner watches TV. The employee who has mastered the art of detail management is indispensable.

It's a fairly easy task to master, yet few people truly manage details well. So let managing the details be one of the details that sets you apart to get ahead.

Follow Through

On the job, there are many opportunities to work on special projects, committees, or boards. Plenty of people will volunteer to do the work. They might think they will actually get it done. They might want to look good in front of others, or they might have made a hasty decision and overestimated their time or skills. Few people actually follow through to do the hard work.

If people can depend on you to follow through, you will be valuable. If your follow through is thoughtful and gets the job done in an intelligent, thorough, meaningful way, you will be invaluable.

Planning is important. Process is necessary. Implementation is where successful organizations (and careers) are built and sustained. Be sure to follow up on your follow through.

Face Time

In meetings it's easy to take a moment to scan the room and view each person around the table. Based on their facial and body expressions, we usually make a determination about what they are thinking. Some look tired while others seem engaged. Some appear angry or frustrated, and others give the impression of great boredom. Sometimes people's countenances reveal exactly what they are thinking or feeling, but often people don't realize the impression they are giving.

Once, after a meeting, a colleague mentioned an intern who looked "incredibly bored" throughout the meeting. Later, the intern said she had no idea what she was doing to give that impression. It involved her chin resting in her hand, dull eyes, and not much reaction to the conversation.

Everyone's resting face is different. Some people smile, some smirk, some frown and wrinkle their brow. It's important to remember that your face is what you use to broadcast your feelings and emotions and is the best shortcut people have to understanding more about you. Make it a habit to mentally note what facial expressions you are making. Just like in poker, use this trick to your advantage.

There are times that you should strategically make the face that will communicate what you need others to understand. Serious discussions require serious reactions. Introductory conversations can be more lighthearted. Learn what is appropriate and develop a strategy for yourself. Your face is one of the greatest communication tools you have, so make it your asset.

Preparation Pays

Keeping up with what is happening at work is necessary. Staying one step ahead is preferable. Fortunately, given the internet and the various social networks that are now available, finding information and doing background research is easy. In fact, it is so easy that you have no excuse for going to a meeting unprepared. The key is to be organized, thorough, and timely about collecting needed data and making needed preparations.

For example, if you are invited to a meeting with your boss and some guests, get an advance list of the attendees and the agenda. Look up each participant so you will be able to put a name and affiliation with each face. Take a few minutes to read about their organizations or firms. Check to see if there are any items or terms on the agenda that you don't understand. If there are, do some research or talk with a trusted colleague before the meeting date.

If you are staffing the meeting, it is usually a good idea to prepare a brief summary along with pictures and titles of participants for your boss. Ask if your boss would like any information packets prepared for distribution. If so, make two or three extra packets in case a participant brings a colleague along.

Check the meeting room well in advance. Everything should be neat and in working order. If a code for wifi is needed, be certain you have it available. If name tents are used, be sure the spelling and credentials are accurate.

If meetings are your responsibility, develop a meeting checklist and use it for every meeting, including small ones. That way no important details are overlooked and embarrassing situations are avoided.

When meetings begin, you may find it helpful to do a discreet seating chart as people introduce themselves. This chart will help prevent your referring to someone by an incorrect name or title. It also will prove useful if you are the person documenting the meeting.

Always make sure you have enough business cards with you. Also, before any meeting starts, think for a few minutes about the best way to introduce yourself for this particular meeting. Can you do so with one short sentence, or will you be prepared, if asked, to say a bit more about your background that is relevant to the meeting? Take your lead from your boss and what others say. You don't want to appear timid nor verbose.

During your professional career, you will attend many meetings that are poorly planned and poorly executed. Every now and then, you will attend one that is well done. Learn from both examples so that meetings you organize and lead are both exceptional and enjoyable. "Be prepared" is not only a motto of the Girl Scouts. It applies to your career, too.

Public Speaking—You Can and You Must

Most professional careers require some public speaking, yet many people claim that they can't do it, that they have an insurmountable fear of giving a talk or presentation before an audience. Public speaking is simply a skill. It can be learned, it can be taught, and it can be mastered.

The most general rule for public speaking is to speak only about things you know. It's not like a college classroom where you are given a random assignment. When the topic is within your area of expertise, your comfort level is much greater. Even so, you need to prepare and practice. Go over your presentation again and again. Read it out loud to be sure it has good transitions and that it flows. Time it. It should be about two minutes less than the time allotted. A shorter presentation will help if the program or your presentation starts a few minutes late.

Make every effort to check the room where you will be speaking in advance of the event. Get there early and, if possible, walk up on the stage. Check the podium, the microphone, and the lighting. Make sure you can read the monitor and advance slides if you are using them.

Keep a presentation journal. Closely observe what outstanding speakers do and make notes about it. How do they open their presentations? How do they handle the question and answer period, especially if a person in the audience disagrees with them? How do they recover if something doesn't work?

Some people suggest you start by telling the audience you are nervous. That may make the listeners more sympathetic toward you, but it also makes you look like an amateur. Don't try to tell a joke or be funny. Leave that to the experts.

Begin small. Keep your standards modest. Remember that it takes practice to do anything well. If you are offered some professional media training, jump at the opportunity, or suggest to your boss that your whole team could benefit from presentation skills training. You will eventually find your own style of public speaking, you will become proficient, and you will wonder why you were ever so nervous about it.

Speak Up Early

You've been in a room full of people where everyone is vying for attention. You've also been in a classroom or a boardroom where some people just won't stop speaking. In these situations, it might seem easy to sit back and not compete for floor space.

In some situations, however, silence may not be the best approach. In fact, when you are part of a work team, the longer you wait to enter the conversation, the harder it may become, especially when you are a woman in a male-dominated group. When you find yourself on a work team, try to enter the conversation as early as you can, preferably within the first ten minutes. What you say doesn't have to be profound. Most of what your colleagues say won't be profound or particularly useful. It can be as simple as saying, "I agree with that assessment," or "We already have some data on that issue," or "Why do you think that?"

Once you speak, you gain the right to speak again, to be part of the ongoing deliberation or debate. By speaking, you make yourself visible, harder to ignore or dismiss as a non-player.

Try speaking up early the next time you are in an important meeting. Don't let your lack of voice lead to a lack of recognition.

Sports Laden Communication

Get the ball rolling, play ball, three strikes and you're out, whole new ball game. Playing hard ball. Step up to the plate, hit it out of the park, batting a thousand. Heavyweight, lightweight, roll with the punches, hitting below the belt, saved by the bell, down for the count, down but not out. Fish or cut bait. Slam dunk. Sudden death overtime. Monday morning quarterback. No holds barred, hole in one, not up to par, the ball's in your court. Run a tight ship, learn the ropes. Go for the gold.

Even if you are not a sports fan, you will recognize most of the phrases above as "sports speak." They are idioms or phrases that have become integrated into common language, especially in the business environment. They are often used as motivational phrases to set goals and strategies. For many men, they are like a shorthand that doesn't need further explanation.

That's not to say there aren't some idioms more closely related to women or drawn from traditional areas like dance or cooking. Phrases such as out of step, doing a song and dance, fancy footwork, piece of cake, half-baked idea, and cook the books come to mind. While most people know their meanings, they aren't as frequently used in the workplace.

If you work in a business environment with many men or a boss who is a man, you probably will have little choice but to adapt to the sports jargon. You don't have to use sports speak yourself, but you do need to understand the meaning of the idioms or you may be disadvantaged during a discussion or meeting.

Think of it like learning a new skill or another language. Game on.

There Are ~~No~~ Stupid Questions

New jobs can be overwhelming, particularly if you are in your first professional position. There can be an immense amount to learn, and it might feel like there is no roadmap. From memorizing your coworkers' names to understanding what is expected of you, work can initially be intimidating.

We have all been in meetings where we understand very little about the discussion. Often our colleagues are speaking quickly and using acronyms that we don't understand. In these circumstances, the old saying that "there are no stupid questions" is highly overrated. If people aren't slowing down to allow time for questions or haven't shown an interest in making sure you understand, they probably won't welcome detailed questions. Much of the time you can Google what you are curious about after the meeting. It's easy to identify organizations, people, or major concepts in your field. If you are lucky, you will have a good supervisor or a helpful mentor whom you can ask questions of later if you really don't understand.

Most people won't mind answering questions that involve complex or nuanced matters. If you have a series of questions that can easily be answered through a bit of research, then find out for yourself before taking someone's time. A good rule of thumb is to thoroughly think about your question before you ask it. Making your boss' job easier is part of your job, and even if it requires a bit of extra work on your own, it will be worth it.

OFFICE ETIQUETTE

Neither a Borrower Nor a Lender Be

We have all read or heard the horror stories about relatives lending or borrowing money. The experts tell us that if it is done at all, it should be done formally with written documents and interest rates. Without these, it becomes easier for the borrower to think of the loan as a gift, or to delay payment. This situation can cause friction among loved ones and can lead to anger, even alienation.

Money issues in the workplace can be equally difficult. The problems can start as simply as someone never having enough cash for lunch and asking a coworker to cover for her until she can get to an ATM. But the repayment doesn't happen. Or, you share a cab and one rider says she has no cash at the moment. In fact, she never has cash, and you get tired of being the one responsible for all the expenses.

Worse yet, perhaps a coworker asks you for a small loan for a few days or just until payday. You know she is struggling financially and, against your better judgment, you decide to help. But payday comes and she conveniently forgets the agreement. It is awkward to have to ask for the repayment, and you feel used. When you finally do confront her, she says doesn't have the money yet, which creates a rift. She avoids you because she is embarrassed she can't pay you, and you are angry at her for taking advantage.

Some coworkers can go back and forth, taking turns and repaying whomever picks up lunch or buys the coffee or pays for the cab. They keep an informal tally and no one feels abused. Anything beyond that is a risk. It simply is never a good idea to lend or borrow money at work.

Relationship Train Wrecks At Work

The chances of finding your soulmate at work are slim. The chances of a work fling or relationship ending and making work awkward and uncomfortable for you and others are high. Romantic relationships at work happen. Some employers are less strict about it than others. However, as a general rule of thumb, they are a bad idea. Whether it is true or not, a relationship with a coworker gives the impression that your focus is not entirely on your work. Even worse, if you're dating someone who is senior to you, it could be perceived that you are receiving preferential treatment.

You will spend a lot of time at your job—probably more than anywhere else. You will form bonds with many of your coworkers and have experiences together that draw you closer to one another. If a relationship does form, it is wise to carefully plan how you handle it. If your employer has policies against dating in the workplace, the repercussions could be serious.

Romantic relationships at work open the door for others to judge you, unfairly or not. Women tend to be judged more harshly than men for such behavior. Work is challenging enough without adding this to the equation. Do your best to avoid it.

Religion In the Workplace

We live in an age where privacy is almost an illusion. Information about our lives is readily available on the internet, and many people underestimate the impact of what they themselves disclose publicly.

When it comes to the workplace, there are still topics that are better kept private. Religion is one of these. While everyone has the right to practice her or his religion, trying to proselytize others or disparaging another's religious beliefs is not acceptable in the office.

Many organizations have written policies about expressing religion. For example, prayer or invocation at meetings or gatherings may be acceptable, but using one religious perspective may not (for instance, praying in the name of Jesus). Using phone messages that end with a religious phrase or adding a Bible verse or religious quote at the bottom of an email is generally not acceptable. Having religious icons displayed in offices or as computer screen savers is regarded generally as unprofessional.

However, it is also useful to spend some time learning about differing religious customs if you are not familiar with them. This is one area where a little knowledge goes a long way. Sensitivity to the significance of religious holidays for various faiths should always be taken into account. Not all employees celebrate Christian holidays, and meetings should not be scheduled on major holidays of other faiths such as Yom Kippur and Ramadan.

Articles of clothing such as the hijab or headscarves for Muslim women or yarmulkes for Jewish men are always acceptable. So is the wearing of a crucifix or cross for Catholics or Protestants.

Awareness of, and sensitivity to, various religious practices results in a diverse and inclusive workplace. Be certain you understand and adhere to workplace policies that address religion.

Small Change and Celebrations

Each workplace has its own culture regarding personal celebrations and gift-giving. Some places see it as an intrusion and a waste of work time. Others are constantly celebrating births, group or individual birthdays, or team successes. You may love these, but if you don't, you will need to find a way to deal with them.

If it's an all staff event, you probably have to at least make an appearance. If your boss is going to be there, you should be there, too. If it's a smaller group, like a birthday cake over lunch, you might want to drop by for a few minutes to offer best wishes.

It gets harder to know where to set suitable boundaries when coworkers collect money for presents for other coworkers. This practice can become expensive for you if carried to the extreme. If you find yourself being consistently asked for donations, you might want to talk to your boss or to the human resources office about it. Or, you can give a modest contribution and think of it as an investment in good will.

Most offices do have policies about selling items or soliciting donations at work. There is always the mother who wants to help her daughter sell Girl Scout cookies, or someone selling raffle tickets for their church, or a colleague who is running in a race for a favorite charity and is looking for sponsorship. You do not have to participate in these fundraisers and politely declining should be sufficient.

The key to managing all of these issues is to be gracious. You will eventually find appropriate ways to avoid celebratory events you don't wish to attend. You may schedule an outside meeting or conference call around the same time so you can skip the event or only attend briefly. Or you can make it known that you only give to certain charities. Also, you can give the colleague a personal card or send a congratulatory email instead of participating in the group event.

You don't want to be excluded from all workplace events or celebrations. You don't want coworkers labeling you as cheap or stand-offish. Instead, you need to find a middle ground that gives you both choice and some personal control.

So Not a Morning Person

We all have our own circadian rhythms. Some people love getting up early, watching the sunrise, and starting the day at the gym before work. Others, though, enjoy watching the moon rise and they get a "second wind" about 10 pm. These are the colleagues who feel they do their best work at night.

Most offices have a usual start and stop time. Unless you work in a position that is divided into shifts, or unless your office is progressive and you can choose when and where you work, these hours are usually 9 to 5. You may be able to flex an hour or so on either side of the day, but generally there are core hours.

If you hate mornings and have a hard time feeling productive early in the day, you might want to time your arrival at work after the coffee and conversation. If you have any control over when to schedule meetings, schedule them later in the day when you are at your best.

If you have to be at work for an early meeting, get up an hour earlier so you have time to ease into your day and you have plenty of time for your commute. Rushing into a meeting late and looking harried and disgruntled may start the meeting and the workday on a sour note.

Most of the work world operates to the benefit of the morning person. If you don't fit this model, you will need to find ways to compensate. Sometimes it's nice to see the sun come up.

Swan In a Ditch

There's a book on profanity in the workplace, a "tongue-in-cheek" manual for how to swear at work without actually using any swear words. Thus the phrase "swan in a ditch." The imagery is fun and recalls phrases used years ago—like "gosh darn it," "dangnabbit," "ticked off," or "oh, heck." While these phrases may still be heard in some parts of the country, most swearing today is more descriptive.

Is it acceptable to swear in today's workplace? A corollary to that question is, is it acceptable for women to swear in the workplace?

There are many issues to consider. For example, does your company have a policy about it? Is it considered disrespectful or intimidating behavior? Could it be construed as creating a hostile work environment?

Next, is your office multigenerational? If so, would coworkers who are the age of your mother or grandmother be comfortable with such language?

Some profanity is offensive to different ethnic or religious groups. Some is gender biased. Some is simply too vulgar or graphic.

There is a wide variance of acceptability of profanity within organizations. Some researchers believe that it enhances cohesiveness and solidarity—that staff need to be comfortable enough to swear. Others claim that it is a good stress reliever, and that, especially when used with humor, it can have a positive impact in a tense situation.

There are several guidelines that might be helpful. First, don't ever swear directly at a coworker or someone who reports to you. Never put profanity in writing, even if writing an email to a close business associate. Once it is out there, it can never be gotten back.

Be aware of, and sensitive to, people who might be offended by your swearing. Observe whether your manager and the boss ever swear in public, or if they are selective about when and where they use profanity. Finally, be especially careful of swearing when you are angry.

One high school English teacher claimed that only people with poor vocabularies resort to profanity. She may have been right.

Talk Is Cheap, Silence Is Golden

Most of us never leave home without our cell phones. We feel lost without them. In fact, many people no longer have land lines. Their cell phones are their main connection for all personal calls. This dependence on having a cell phone creates some new problems in the workplace.

Depending on your position, you may also be issued a work phone to be used for business purposes only. That means you must carry two phones and that doubles your chance of having a call interrupt a meeting.

Hearing someone's phone, especially a cutesy ring tone, during a presentation or discussion is rude and irritating. Usually there is a mumbled apology or the receiver rushes out of the room to take or silence the call.

Unless you work in a job that deals in emergencies, there is no excuse for a phone to ever ring during a meeting. The best thing is to leave your phone(s) in your office or cubicle. All calls can go to voice mail so you can return them at a more appropriate time.

If you are expecting an important call that you can't miss, put your phone on vibrate and sit as near the door as possible. Slip out quietly to take the call and return as quickly as you can.

Some employees fail to realize how offensive it is to take a call or to be texting when in a meeting. It is disrespectful to your boss or a presenter. Many bosses won't tolerate cell phone interruptions or your inattention. You may be surprised if your boss publicly asks you to turn off your phone. You'll be even more embarrassed if she tells you to leave the meeting. No phone call is worth that.

Teach Them Well

Chances are that you interned before landing your first professional position. You probably were eager to please and fit in with your supervisor and the employees at your agency. Most interns feel accomplished and mature when starting an internship and don't see themselves much different from those who actually receive a paycheck. However, there are, in fact, clear differences between being an intern and being an employee.

When you start your career, there will probably be interns at your place of employment. They will most likely be just a few years younger than you are. However, there is still a power differential between you and them, and you have to draw clear boundaries. It is inappropriate for you to have a friendship outside of work (and certainly not a romantic relationship) with interns at your organization. You can be friendly with, or positive towards, interns. They are there to learn, and you can certainly be a resource to help teach them. They may be the first people to view you as an expert and to show admiration towards you for your professional standing. It can be tempting to let their awe go to your head.

Your goal (particularly in your first professional job) is to produce quality work and gain respect from your boss and your colleagues. If you spend all your time associating with interns, you will probably be viewed as one. Maintain appropriate relationships and help interns do what they are there to do—learn.

The Walls Have Ears

Today, thanks to cell phones, we are constantly surrounded by conversations. People talk while they are walking, shopping, and eating. It seems like there are no longer filters on language used or content discussed. If nearby, you can listen to the intricacies of a legal matter or the intimacies of a personal relationship.

This same behavior can be observed in the office. Though a conversation you're having may seem harmless, it can have damaging effects. For example, perhaps you use profanity when speaking to friends or arguing with a family member, but disrespectful language is not acceptable in your setting. People may be surprised to hear the negative way you speak to others and that could change their good opinion of you.

Conversely, coworkers should not be privy to your personal communication with your significant other or fiancé. Your personal life is none of their business and, at worst, overhearing even one side of a conversation filled with sexual innuendo is awkward and inappropriate at work.

Damage to your organization may also occur. Often employees don't think about who is hearing their conversations in elevators, in the cafeteria, while waiting for a meeting to start, or in a public venue. You may not know trade secrets, but you may be working on a grant proposal or trying to recruit a new customer or hire an employee in which competitors are interested. Your overheard remarks may give them an advantage.

Perhaps even worse, you may be complaining about what a jerk your boss is, and her boss is in the back of the elevator. Or her husband had just dropped by to meet your boss for lunch and overhears your remarks. These overhead remarks can create disastrous situations for you.

In many settings like health care or law offices, divulging confidential information in any format will result in termination of your employment. So always be certain your private communication is truly private and always publicly appropriate.

Timing Is Everything

"If you're early, you're on time. If you're on time, you're late." Not everyone abides by this rule, but people who really care about time and punctuality are strict about it. If you have a boss or senior colleague who is sensitive to time, you will do harm to your reputation by not being at meetings and events a few minutes early.

When you show up late, you broadcast that you think your time is more valuable than everyone else's time. Inevitably, we will all run into unforeseen circumstances like a flat tire or a sick child, but it's important to take every precaution to not be late.

Leave extra early. Set several alarm clocks. Pick your clothes out the night before. Select a breakfast that doesn't take a long time to prepare. Arriving 30 minutes early gives you time to prepare, settle your nerves if you're anxious, and appear professional. Arriving late will not only fluster you, but will also annoy others.

OFFICE POLITICS

A Grain of Salt

Along your career path, you will be offered advice. Some will be helpful, some will be terrible, some will be unsolicited, some will be offensive, and some you will never forget. When you begin your career, you are likely hungry for guidance and willing to take help where you can find it.

People may give you advice that is in direct contradiction with the advice you receive from someone else. People will give you advice that may make no sense at the time, but that will come in handy one day. It is up to you to sort through this advice and determine which pieces you will apply to your career.

Typically, if you respect someone and look to them as a role model, that is a good person from whom to take advice. Sometimes it will come from surprising places, and you should be open to hearing what others have to offer. However, manipulation can also come in the form of "advice."

Take it all with a grain of salt and do what makes you comfortable. It's your career, and no one else is going to make the important decisions for you.

Beware the Lemmings

The lemming is a small rodent that mostly lives in the Arctic. Folklore has it that lemmings follow each other even when it results in their jumping off cliffs in what some describe as mass suicides.

The lemming analogy is a cautionary tale for a "group think" mentality and can be applied to several situations in the workplace. New employees are more susceptible to becoming lemmings than others who are better informed.

Frequently, an established worker volunteers to help the new person get settled. This dynamic can be useful—or not. They can show you where to find things, introduce you to others, and offer to become your lunch companion. This phenomenon might be similar to first meeting your roommate in college. Because of proximity, and because you didn't know many people, you became friends of convenience. As you met more people, your dependence on your roommate may have declined as you realized you didn't have as much in common as you thought.

It is important to take your time forming friendships or habits in the workplace. During your first few weeks, try to meet and get to know as many people as you can. It is fine to have lunch with someone or with a group, but keep in mind that it may be difficult to extricate yourself from the group later on if you are not compatible or you don't share many common interests.

There is always an interest in the new girl. Others may fish for information or ask you directly about your salary or benefits, whether you have a partner, or what you think of the boss. Limiting self-disclosure in the workplace is generally advised, but it is even more important when you first begin employment as you may unwittingly become a pawn in office politics.

Also be cautious about participating in gossip or accepting someone else's assessment of other employees or your boss. Reserve judgment until you can form your own opinions.

Finally, take time to review operational policies and adhere to them despite encouragement by others to bend the rules. If you have an hour for lunch, be back at your desk in an hour even if your colleagues always take 90 minutes. Don't lend someone your security card or show them a memo from your supervisor. A simple statement such as, "I'm sorry but I'm not comfortable doing that," should suffice as an explanation.

It will take some time, but you will become comfortable in your new organization. If you focus on being conscientious and on doing the best job you can, the other issues should fall into place without you falling over the cliff.

Dependable to Indispensable

New professionals may underestimate the importance of being dependable. Dependable may sound dull and unexciting, but it often forms the cornerstone from which careers grow. Dependability is the first step toward indispensability

Dependability refers to numerous interrelated traits and behaviors. It means whether your boss and coworkers can count on you—all of the time, every time. It means you get to work when you should, that you stay as long as necessary to get the job done, and that your absences are few, necessary, and scheduled. It means you arrive at every meeting well prepared. It means you do your part on all assignments and that you can be counted on to share the credit or to accept responsibility as part of the team when something doesn't work.

But dependability goes further than simply following workplace policies or exhibiting appropriate business behavior. For example, is your input always constructive? Do you regularly volunteer for assignments or to help with special projects or problems?

Dependability also includes personal traits. Can your boss depend on your integrity, your honesty, your fairness, and your confidentiality? Can she count on you being positive despite significant problems or workplace chaos? Can she count on you to anticipate her needs?

If you can answer "yes" to the above, you have laid the foundation for being an asset not only for your boss, but also for your organization.

Deal With It or Get Over It

There are few things more obnoxious than passive aggressiveness, particularly in the workplace. Either address the problem you are having with your colleague or let it go. Don't silently fume, talk badly about someone behind her back, or let emails or phone calls go unanswered.

Being passive aggressive means you've stooped to a level that is beneath you. It is immature. Sometimes the person you are "punishing" may have no idea what she's done to offend you. If you respectfully bring it to her attention, she may apologize and you both can move on. She may also be defensive or angry, but at least you've done your part in terms of acknowledging the problem. People tend to get more respect for bringing tough problems out into the open, rather than walking around with a chip on their shoulder. Usually just acknowledging your frustration is enough to enable you to let go of the anger that you've been holding inside.

It's also a good idea to try to resolve an issue with your coworker before it escalates to your supervisor or human resources. It is the respectful and diplomatic way of addressing a situation. Then, if something can't be rectified one on one, at least you had the courage to discuss it with your colleague before seeking intervention. You can depend on these colleagues who you know will be honest with you, and you won't have to worry about hurt feelings or misunderstandings festering and potentially poisoning projects.

If you cannot, or will not, address an issue, you have to let it go. Perhaps it's too hard to confront a certain person, your workplace is not conducive to any kind of conflict, or you are fearful that your job could be affected. Then you have to let it go. That is your only choice. People will get tired of hearing you groan about it, your resentment will consume you, and, ultimately, it will only hurt you. Step up to the plate or walk away.

Drawing Boundaries

One of the hardest things to remember on the job is that all people are out for themselves, or they should be. We all want to do a good job—whether it's so we can best serve our clients, make sure our organization succeeds, earn a higher salary or a promotion, or simply because we have an ego to feed.

A lesson hard learned for many is that it's usually not wise to put blind faith in people. Don't entirely trust your colleagues. This doesn't mean that they aren't kind and worthy people. It does mean that sometimes juicy information is too hard to keep to themselves. Sometimes you and your colleagues will compete for a job. Sometimes people will stab you in the back. If your coworker is gossiping about someone in your office, why wouldn't she gossip about you? If you've opened yourself up to let these things happen, then don't be surprised when they do.

We all find the balance that makes us comfortable. Some disclose nothing personal and can come off as cold and callous. It's nearly impossible to not engage with your coworkers on some personal level, simply to be polite, if nothing else. Others compulsively overshare and become the office joke. Your colleagues don't need to know what you did this weekend when you had too much to drink. Even if they don't say anything, people are most likely silently logging their judgments about your behavior. Your family, friends, and partner are more appropriate outlets for your dreams, fears, pet peeves, disappointments, and successes. Draw a line between the personal and professional. That line is an invisible, but important, step to advocating for yourself by not revealing too much information.

Friend In Fair Weather—Or a Hurricane

Errors are common in the workplace. If the error is small, an employee can recover from it quite easily. Perhaps only a supervisor or a work team will ever know it occurred. Really big screw-ups are harder because they are generally visible to everyone, and they can have disastrous consequences. These types of mistakes usually work their way up through the chain of command. Sometimes they have high external visibility or require the involvement of legal counsel.

Perhaps an employee missed an important deadline, and the organization lost the funding source for a grant. Or a miscalculation or payment of some invoice caused an internal or external audit. Other errors may attract media attention, and a public apology might be required from the employee and/or the CEO. Maybe the issue was a workplace altercation or argument that triggered a grievance or a serious enough error that it resulted in a law suit. Or perhaps the employee was involved in some external event that was considered a conflict of interest such as using company letterhead for a political cause.

Some errors may be so significant the employee simply can't recover. They may be fired or given the option to resign. Other errors, though, may only require a letter to their file, or the employee may be placed on probation for a certain period of time.

If your coworker or friend is responsible for a workplace mistake, try your best to be supportive. Too often, others start avoiding the individual because they are afraid they will be judged less competent by association. Also, sometimes one employee is singled out as responsible, but it was a group effort or the error should have been caught at the next level. If one employee is made the scapegoat, others who were implicit in any way may try to distance themselves from the coworker so they can distance themselves from the error.

Making a mistake that others know about is embarrassing enough. Feeling like friends and coworkers no longer support you is hurtful, even devastating. None of us will go through our careers error free, so bank some good karma for when it's your turn to be in the hot seat and do your best to help your colleague recover her standing.

Gossip Girl

Unless you work from home, or are on your own for a good portion of time, office gossip will be an inevitable reality of your workday. Every environment is different, but as long as humans interact on the job, they will talk about one another. It's not always negative. Sometimes people will be impressed by a colleague and sing her praises. Sometimes office talk will be seemingly innocuous like an update about someone's project. However, sometimes it is negative. When you are together for over eight hours each day, idiosyncrasies emerge, passions flare, and, sometimes, personalities clash. Add to this that work is serious business because it involves people's reputations and livelihoods, and it can be a recipe for disaster.

You might feel like you're bonding with colleagues who are hungry for chatter. People often trade banter and perhaps you don't want to feel left out. Maybe it's even your boss engaging in inappropriate gossip, and you feel obligated to respond. Be careful, though, because negative comments involving coworkers can inevitably backfire. You might be the target of gossip, or a colleague you thought you could trust will tell others about your private conversations.

We are all put in this position, and it's difficult to stay above the fray. Ask yourself if what you are saying was broadcast to all of your colleagues, would you be embarrassed or regretful? If so, then chances are you should keep it to yourself. Excuse yourself from conversations that take a turn towards gossip or find a tactful way to change the conversation.

Keeping Secrets

It happens to most of us. We accidentally mention or tell something to someone and then think better of it. We ask them to keep the issue or item confidential.

Disclosing personal or business information that you don't want others to know is a risk in the workplace. People usually intend to keep your confidences, but the temptation to tell others is great. Even close colleagues can trip up. Gossip is a common feature of workplace life, and information is sometimes equated with power. Additionally, if your secret involves a business matter, you may put others at risk if they are asked directly if they have knowledge of a situation.

It is also risky to tell others if you are thinking about applying for a different position, changing jobs, or simply that you can't stand your boss. These remarks can take on a life of their own and can sabotage your career path.

In a similar fashion, it is important to think carefully before agreeing to keep a secret for a coworker. Depending on the nature of the information, there are times withholding knowledge might not be possible, or you might accidentally breach the confidence, or you find that not disclosing it puts you in a difficult position.

Secrets can be hard to manage. As the adage goes: "If you want it to be a secret, don't tell anyone."

One of the Boys

Women may feel disadvantaged by an "old boys' network" at the office. We know that many deals get done on the golf course or at the gym or at a bar after work. It can make you wonder if and how you should try to be included in these activities. Sometimes, the easiest route appears to be the drink. This tactic is not foolproof, however, and you should consider possible consequences.

Joining a mixed group of coworkers and having a glass of wine or a drink is generally acceptable. More than that, though, and you might find yourself being too talkative or flirtatious or acting in an unprofessional manner. And think how rumors would spread through the office if someone had to drive you home or put you in a taxi because you had had too much to drink.

It ups the ante even further if your boss is present. All types of scenarios can happen, and not all of them are good. While you may find it useful to get to know the boss a little better, there are some potential risks. For example, how do you handle the situation if your boss has too much to drink and acts unprofessionally? Worse yet, what do you do if he or she propositions you? This can have a disastrous impact.

Like other social situations, you need to find ways to graciously handle the after work invitation, particularly if it seems to be an office routine. You can stop by every now and then, perhaps with a friend or coworker. You can say you don't drink and turn down the invitation. Or you can explain that you car pool or have a standing obligation after work.

It's not that you really want to be "one of the boys" or to be considered "a good time girl." What you do want is to be treated equally in the workplace and to maintain your professional reputation at all times.

Stress Carriers

We all know one or two of them. They may be a friend, relative, or coworker. What they have in common is that they scatter stress like Tinkerbell scatters fairy dust. They are stress carriers. They often appear friendly and helpful, but they have a knack—and perhaps the intention—of making others feel inadequate or upset. They also are skillful at shifting their work or worries to others so smoothly that you are left wondering how it happened.

It is easy to recognize a stress carrier by your reaction to him or her. You tense up each time they approach, and you are relieved when they move on. Or, you may find yourself puzzled by how you ended up with a new task or assignment, especially when the person is not in a position to delegate. This trick is a tribute to their manipulation talents.

The best approach is to avoid the stress carrier whenever possible. In the workplace, however, avoidance may prove difficult. If you are too negative, you can appear hostile or uncooperative. At the same time, you don't want them to take advantage of you.

Humor can work. So can being a bit more direct. Saying something like, "Are you trying to shift your work to me again?" may be effective if said in a teasing or pleasant manner.

Changing how you react is another option. If you can recognize the situation, you can erect an emotional stress barrier to the stress carrier. Creating effective barriers may take some practice, but it is well worth the effort.

CHARACTER CULTIVATION

Care Less

Little girls are taught to get along with others. They are "sugar and spice and everything nice," and told not to rock the boat. They are polite and pleasing to others. They are often described as cute, sweet, or well-behaved. Meanwhile, little boys learn that it's generally accepted for them to question, fight, and be more aggressive. Proper manners are encouraged in most children, but expected more from girls.

While it seems harmless enough, these societal standards end up putting girls and women at a disadvantage. Many women shy away from conflict and try to keep the peace, which can be an admirable quality. However, in order to get ahead, you are probably going to have to step on a few toes. That means being assertive, standing your ground, and pushing back when necessary. Being a kind, decent person is important, but being a pushover is unacceptable on the road to getting your name on the door.

At the end of the day, you cannot lose sleep over what others think of you. This doesn't mean that you can throw caution to the wind and behave carelessly. It does mean, however, that you literally have to care less about people-pleasing for the sake of avoiding conflict. Opinions and criticisms of you cannot constantly influence your decisions, actions, or self-worth. Otherwise, you will be continuously pushed in one direction and then pulled in another. You will look weak and others will take advantage of you. Be confident in your work and stand by your decisions.

Event Survival

Many after-hour work events, such as dinners and galas, are simply an extension of the work day. That doesn't mean they can't be enjoyable, but they do take time, energy, and preparation. Some people thrive on the social interaction of such events. They see it as an opportunity to make contacts, to be noticed, or to get a photograph with an important colleague or celebrity. Others see these events as tedious and time consuming.

If you are just beginning your professional career and find yourself being asked to attend social events related to your job, you will need to develop a personal system for event survival. You don't always get a choice about what you attend. Your boss may ask you to accompany her or you may be asked to go in her place. If you are sent to represent your organization, what happens if you don't know anyone? A room full of people can feel overwhelming when you are alone at an event. If you have a tendency for shyness, it can be even more difficult.

There are a few things that might help you become more comfortable. First, be sure to take time to prepare. Look up the sponsoring organization and its leaders. Put a list of important names and pictures in your phone. It is easy to discreetly check your phone while at an event.

Next, be sure you understand the reason for the event and why you are being asked to attend. Is it simply to fill a seat at a company table, or are you being asked to seek out someone and introduce yourself, or to make apologies for your boss's absence? One of the easiest ways to interact in a room of people you don't know is to introduce yourself to someone who is standing alone. They may feel as uncomfortable as you do and usually will be grateful for the conversation. Come armed with a few general opening questions such as, "What is your relationship to the sponsoring organization?"

It's always a good idea to limit alcohol when you are working an event. While it might make you feel more at ease, it can also make you too chatty or too bold. You don't want someone reporting to your boss that you were the life of the party.

As you gain experience in your professional field you will find that you know a greater number of people, and event attendance will become less trying. Until then, prepare for a work-related social event like it is part of your job. Because it is.

It's Not Fair

Life is not fair. Those of us who grew up with siblings probably complained that someone got the bigger half of the candy bar, got to stay out later, or got better treatment. We saw lack of fairness continue in school or sports or in the neighborhood.

Eventually, we came to realize that life isn't always fair. We accepted that fact, and now we usually don't dwell on it. Sometimes, though, you may find yourself in a work environment where fairness is called into question. There may be discrepancies in salaries, promotions, assignments, or work shifts. Your boss may have favorites. Someone may be identified as a "golden" employee and be given every opportunity to shine. Others may take credit for your work or try to undercut your reputation.

It's important to recognize what is truly unfair and what you might be using as an excuse for not doing your best work. It's also important to recognize what you can change and what amount of unfairness you can tolerate. Try to deal with each situation directly, professionally, and factually. Humor can be useful. Likewise, having a confidential conversation with a mentor might help. If an unfair situation gets too difficult for you to manage or work around, changing jobs may be the only solution.

On the other hand, be certain you aren't part of the problem. Make sure you are performing at a high level and doing your share of the work. Be flexible and helpful. Become a team player and keep your competitive spirit under control. Most importantly, give credit when and where you should. Situations may be unfair, but you don't have to be.

Kindness Is Not Weakness

If you were asked to name a mean teacher in school or a mean boss, you probably could do so without thinking very hard. You could easily describe why they were mean. Perhaps they made hurtful comments to others, or they were belittling, or caustic. Maybe they were rude and antagonistic. Probably children or employees were somewhat afraid of them and did their best to avoid them and keep out of their way.

Like labeling in general, once a label is attached to an individual, it is hard to change. The person's behavior is almost always viewed through the lens of that label.

Kindness doesn't take much time or effort. It doesn't require personal disclosure or crossing professional boundaries. It doesn't mean you have to have a bubbly personality or spend much time or money. What it does require is common courtesy and genuineness.

Kindness can be as simple as acknowledging the custodians and person at the security desk, thanking someone who does something for you, or offering congratulations when someone earns recognition or is promoted. It means offering sympathy when someone has experienced a loss or offering assistance when a coworker is struggling with an assignment under a deadline.

Kindness can take the form of encouragement when someone has made a mistake or support when someone is under fire. Kindness can cause you to suspend your initial judgment and give someone the benefit of the doubt. It means refraining from making negative comments even if they may be warranted, or speaking to an employee or coworker in private instead of criticizing them in front of others.

Those in the early stages of their careers may worry that kindness will be perceived as weakness. In fact, kindness is often viewed as a strength, as an indication that individuals are mature and self-secure. Also on the plus side, kindness is usually returned to you just when you need it most.

Loose Cannon Liability

Bosses and supervisors often get requests for recommendations. They have had lots of experiences with different personality types and work ethics, but one of the most confounding is the smart and competent, yet unpredictable, employee. Prone to outbursts and the belief that they know best, these loose cannons may have inappropriate senses of humor and an unwillingness to learn from their mistakes. Feedback on their unacceptable behavior usually results in excuses and shifting blame. Though they are sharp and intelligent, these employees usually don't get good recommendations, nor should they.

You can be the smartest person in the world, but if you are a liability, it doesn't matter. Most bosses would take a smart person who is appropriate and respectful over an unpredictable genius every time. If you make your boss nervous or uneasy, you will find yourself sitting in a cubicle all day without any increased responsibility or freedom. You will be lucky to keep your job.

Make It Match

You spent hours working on your résumé. You attended a seminar, talked to a placement agency, and asked friends, colleagues, and family members for input. The advice you received at times seemed confusing and contradictory. Some said include your GPA. Others said include your hobbies or special interests or personality traits. Everyone said you needed to look tech savvy.

At times, you felt like you were walking a thin line between reality and embellishment. When trying to match your skill set with the job requirements, you found yourself using terms like "proficient" rather than "familiar" with a computer application, or you noted your strong interpersonal skills when you actually struggle with shyness.

You have been told that the résumé is simply a screening tool. The objective is to get an interview and get your foot in the door, but that's not completely accurate. Your résumé becomes a permanent part of your employee record. Falsifying a résumé or job application can be grounds for dismissal if your employer finds that you have not been honest. Equally damaging is not being able to perform work assignments or tasks because you lack the necessary skills—the skills you claimed on your résumé.

Most organizations have a probationary period. During that time, new employees can be terminated without cause and with no severance. You don't want to set yourself up for failure in a new job. You don't want to be in a constant state of anxiety for fear that your boss will ask you to perform some task or function for which you lack the qualifications.

When looking for a job, first take a hard look at your résumé. Make sure it reads well. Make certain it is free of errors. Most importantly, make sure it accurately reflects what you are capable of doing.

Not In the Mood

Not everyone has a sunny personality. Not everyone can be described as nice or friendly. Some people thrive on being negative and finding problems in every event. You know colleagues like this. They never seem to notice the humor in a situation. They relish commenting on problems. Their favorite phrases are, "Yes, but," and, "I told you so."

These coworkers are difficult to be around. They might be very smart but they rarely add anything constructive. They watch team members flounder when they have the answer or when they could help rescue the situation.

Eventually, they earn labels such as "unhappy" and "disgruntled" or "moody" and "downright mean." Coworkers may be reluctant to challenge them or their ideas for fear of a negative diatribe, but they don't respect them. Everyone wonders why they stay in their position or in the organization when they seem so miserable, and colleagues quietly celebrate when they do leave.

You don't want to turn into this person. You may be having a less than perfect day or week, but that doesn't give you the right to be moody in the workplace. If you find yourself saying, "Yes, but" on a regular basis, consider why you are using that approach. Stop yourself from making nasty or snide comments about the efforts of your colleagues, and never resort to personal attacks or insults.

Outlooks, like nicknames, have a way of sticking, of finding their way onto your evaluation form, and even following you from job to job. Getting ahead in the work world is hard enough and broadcasting a bad attitude will make it even harder.

Owners vs. Takers

Ownership is very important in the workplace, and it goes both ways. Employees should take credit, and be rewarded, for good work. However, one of the most commendable qualities an individual can have is to own their work and choices when they make a mistake or something goes wrong. When you figure out that something has gone awry, the best step is to immediately determine what you can do to clean up the mess and resolve the problem. Remain calm and figure out what you need to do to fix it.

Your boss needs to know about any serious problems as quickly as possible, and you have to perform triage to alleviate the emergency. If you are at a loss for what to do, ask your boss for help. It is far better to identify a problem so that you can quickly fix it, than to let your boss be surprised by something negative. Don't blame. Don't equivocate. Don't make excuses. Don't get defensive.

Likewise, don't take credit for other people's work, but offer generous accolades to colleagues for a job well done. When people have worked together long enough, they generally will be able to recognize each other's work product and pinpoint specific styles. When someone takes credit for work that they did not actually do, it appears pathetic, and they become untrustworthy. They will gain no friends and will be transparent to those they are trying to fool.

Put It Behind You

We all have them—bad days at work. We don't do our best. We say things that are stupid, or our colleagues say stupid things to us. We don't take responsibility for mistakes or we don't take credit for a success.

When a bad day happens, you might find yourself being competitive, petty or angry all day. You go over and over the slight or the disagreement. It goes home with you and comes back with you the next day.

When you can't put an event behind you, it saps your strength and clouds your judgment. It can undermine your self-confidence or your professionalism. However, holding on to a bad day is simply a waste of time and energy.

Put issues and errors in perspective. Much of what consumes us on a daily basis is forgotten in a few days. Put them behind you. In the long run, you will discover they were unimportant anyway.

Safer, Not Sorry

Everyone makes mistakes, personally and professionally. They can be minor, such as grammatical errors in a memo, or major, like not hearing your alarm clock and arriving late to an important meeting. Most honest mistakes will be forgiven. In these instances, an apology to your boss or colleagues is appropriate.

However, it crosses a line when you are constantly behaving in ways that require apologies. You can't act irrationally or angrily, and then believe that a simple apology is going to wipe the slate clean. It's far better to think before you act and have nothing to apologize for. People will begin to tune you out because your cycle becomes predictable. Your actions will not be taken seriously and neither will your apology. The best case scenario is that you will become a non-entity. The worst is that people will become so fed up with you that you might be shut out of important work projects and events, or even worse, let go, because of your behavior.

Think about what you are going to say or do before you speak. If it's going to require an apology later, it's best to keep your mouth shut.

BOSS MANAGEMENT

Getting an "A" In the Workplace

We frequently use the phrase "Type A" to refer to someone who seems driven or intense, someone controlling. Years ago, two researchers named Rosenman and Friedman coined the phrase to describe a constellation of personality traits that could lead to early heart disease. The Type A behavior pattern was the riskiest type. Type A personalities have what Rosenman and Friedman describe as "hurry sickness." They live by the clock and a schedule. They generally walk fast, talk fast, and eat fast. They don't waste anyone's time, and they certainly don't want you wasting theirs.

These traits are often rewarded in the workplace, and many individuals who rise to positions of leadership are Type A. Therefore, many bosses fall into this category. If your boss is a Type A (but you are not), you will need to adapt to her personality. Fortunately, Type A's are simple to understand if you do the easy work of accepting their intense personalities and go from there. Earning an "A" grade from a Type A boss requires more than simple good work.

Always be prepared for meetings. Be succinct in your overviews, reports, questions, and answers. Stay focused on the task at hand. Be certain you make deadlines. Don't expect to engage in small talk, and don't be insulted if they appear abrupt. Try to anticipate what they might need or expect, and never be late for a meeting or appointment. In fact, if your boss is a true Type A, she or he will arrive for most meetings a few minutes early and will be annoyed waiting for people who don't arrive until the last minute.

The above habits are good ones to acquire in any work setting, but when you work for a Type A boss, they are essential.

To be successful in your workplace, it is important to know what is expected of you. You should have a job description and receive an orientation when you begin. However, the subtleties of the job you have to learn for yourself if you want to get ahead. Being able to identify whether or not you have a Type A boss and using these tips will help you bypass simple mistakes so you can stay in the fast lane and successfully drive your career.

Fear No Feedback

Honest feedback is a gift. The vast majority of people won't care, or be comfortable, enough to provide helpful, constructive feedback to you. Whether it's in the form of your official evaluation, an assessment from your mentor, or a simple comment from a colleague, be open to the message. You may not agree with it, but you should not be defensive. Be mature enough to handle their critique. If you don't understand where the person is coming from, take the opportunity to analyze your behavior, words, and actions, and figure out why you are being perceived in a certain way. Be curious, ask questions, and try to see yourself through the eyes of others. Accept people's well-intentioned efforts to help you perform better.

If criticism is constant or crosses the line into harassment or ill-will, you have a right to push back. Just be careful in figuring out people's intentions. For the most part, if someone is taking the time to offer commentary on your work, it's because she wants to help you. However, make sure you get feedback from a variety of sources. Seek it out and determine what is useful and what to discard. It will help you to form a thicker skin and will give you insight into yourself that most people don't have. These qualities are essential for leaders.

Groupies Are For Rock Stars, Not Bosses

We should all be so lucky to have impressive bosses—individuals who are smart, dynamic, and innovative and who take an interest in our careers and serve as role models. Unfortunately, bosses with all those qualifications are rare.

Sometimes, however, you may find your boss attractive in a variety of ways. He or she may be physically attractive to you. Or, you may be a bit awed by their brilliance or status. Power itself can be attractive. The individual may have many qualities that you admire, and you may enjoy being around or talking with her.

Keep in mind, though, that what you need from your boss is mutual respect. You don't want to appear juvenile or fawning. You don't want your boss to think you have a crush, that you are flirting, or that you are seeking a personal relationship with her or him. You also don't want to be mistaken for a handmaiden, arm candy, or a groupie.

Some bosses thrive on adoration. They like having followers and like to travel with assistants or staff who are at their beck and call. Think about the politician who enters the room with four or five assistants—usually young and attractive. While initially that may seem exciting to a new employee, it is generally not a pathway to professional success, and, at worst, it may cause an embarrassing or compromising situation for you.

Be noticed for your job performance, not for the fact that you hang on every word or that you are flirtatious. Dress and act professionally so that you are treated professionally. Remember your goal is to be the boss someday.

Idiosyncratic

Everyone has idiosyncrasies including you and your boss. Savvy business people notice others' idiosyncrasies and adjust. It may seem trite, but if your boss hates gum chewing, nail biting, pen tapping, nose sniffing or use of the word "like" or "um," make sure you don't do any of these things. If lateness infuriates your boss, always be early. If your supervisor really values appearance, don't show up to work with wet hair and unkempt clothing. If tattoos disgust her, keep yours hidden. For clean freaks, keep your office tidy. If your boss is not a morning person, save your questions for the afternoon. If your boss is a germaphobe, don't show up to work sick. If she doesn't think kids have a place at work, don't bring yours into the office. If manners are incredibly important to her, don't ever talk with your mouth full and make sure you always say "please and thank you." If strong scents make her sick, tone down the perfume. If she hates cigarettes, you better never smell like an ashtray or take excessive smoke breaks. It may even be as serious as working for a boss who is a recovering alcoholic, and not drinking around her out of respect.

When you work for someone for a decent amount of time, their preferences will become obvious. They will either blatantly tell you, complain in your presence, or you will learn what their facial expressions and body language mean. There's no reason to unnecessarily irritate your boss when you can take simple steps to keep her happy.

It Was So Embarrassing

In the workplace, there are some hard and fast rules that should never be broken. It goes without saying that you should never get in an argument with your boss, especially in front of others. Even when discussing a hot topic, you can't raise your voice or swear. You know you should never lie or withhold important information, and most bosses don't like to be surprised about a work issue.

Less obvious, but no less important, is behaving in a way that embarrasses your boss. This type of error occurs most frequently at meetings. You might think the boss has misspoken and decide to show what you know by providing the correct information. Sometimes in your eagerness to speak, you may talk over or interrupt what your boss is saying. Even worse yet, you might correct your boss's misuse of a word or his or her grammar. Before you speak at a business meeting with your boss present, stop and think for a moment about your comment and your tone. Whether your boss is the unflappable or excitable type, you always want to appear calm and reasoned.

Even without speaking, there are other ways you can embarrass your boss. Being inattentive is one of them. If you sit in a meeting constantly checking your smartphone or using your iPad, you look like you are bored and that the meeting isn't worth your time. No matter how dull the meeting, if your boss is there or the boss asked you to attend, it's worth your time.

Forgetting to turn off your cell phone and having it ring during the meeting can be embarrassing as well as disruptive. At best, it makes you appear forgetful, at worst, self-important.

If you are responsible for providing background materials or packets of information for meeting attendees, be sure they are complete and error free and that there are enough to go around. If your boss will be using slides or media or patching people in by conference call, check the equipment before the meeting begins. Nothing derails a meeting faster than not being ready and appearing disorganized. Even if the details are someone else's responsibility, being unprepared reflects on your boss.

Finally, make certain you are appropriately dressed for the business occasion. The night before, you should double-check your schedule for the next day so that you can plan the right clothes for meetings or events. Showing up inappropriately dressed because you forgot about a meeting or event reflects poorly on you, your boss, and your company.

One thing is certain about embarrassing your boss in public—she or he will probably embarrass you right back either in front of the group or, you hope, in private afterwards.

Get to the Point

Remember that professor who droned on and on? You had trouble staying awake in his class. The course content was okay. The subject was fairly interesting. The problem was that the professor included detail after detail, more than you could take in or would ever need. In your mind, you kept saying, "Get to the point."

In the workplace, you will find coworkers analogous to that professor. Once they get the floor, they don't want to give it up. Their questions—more like a loosely formed commentary or treatise—ramble on until no one is listening any longer. Eventually, someone is able to end the torture, and the meeting moves on.

Individual conversations with this type of coworker usually begin by them declaring, "This will only take a minute." You know that is an underestimation, and you immediately start thinking about how to extricate yourself.

The ability to net it out, to quickly get to the main point, is a good trait to develop. You want to appear organized in your thinking, and you want to be succinct and clear in your comments or presentation. This is especially true when meeting with a supervisor or the boss. Put all extraneous information in a back-up memo and use your time for the important points or "the ask." You don't want to be like that old professor and have your superiors say, "Please get to the point."

No Play, All Work

Traveling to an out of town meeting can be a nice break and a welcome networking opportunity. The dynamics can change, however, if you are attending the meeting with your boss, especially if you are there as administrative back-up.

No matter how long the meetings go or what activities are included, keep in mind that you are at work. Even arranged leisure time activities must be viewed as business. Keep alcohol use to a minimum or forgo it altogether even if your boss is having a few drinks.

Being on time for the meeting is critical. After you get registered, check the layout of the hotel. It's often helpful to find the meeting room in advance. Some hotels are linked to convention centers and rooms can be tricky to locate.

When you get to your hotel room, be certain you have everything you need for getting ready in the morning. If you use a hairdryer, make sure there is one in the room and that it works. It can easily take 20-30 minutes for housekeeping to deliver one if you can't find one in the room when you need it. Check to be sure you understand how the alarm works. If you are especially tired, you might want to set the alarm as well as ask for a wake-up call. It could be disastrous if you oversleep and your boss must wait for you to load his presentation.

Always get to the meeting room early. If you or your boss will be presenting, try and meet the A/V team and ask if there is anything they need from you. Run through the slides if you have the chance. Check the podium to see if there are any concerns. This preparation is important if your boss is the presenter, but it is especially essential if you are the presenter.

Always carry at least one extra hard copy of the presentation and one or two extra flash drives. The boss may accidentally leave his in the restaurant during breakfast, or a colleague may ask for a copy of it after the talk.

Many employees dread traveling with their boss. They feel they have to be on good behavior every minute and that there is too much possibility of something going wrong. Others, however, see it as a great opportunity to interact with the boss on a more personal level, and to help the boss learn more about their skills, ideas, and competency.

Only the Boring

One of your main goals at work should be to make your boss's job easier. There is a simple way to accomplish that seemingly daunting goal and that is anticipating what your boss and your organization will need to get done and setting out to accomplish it. An outstanding response to the interview question, "Why should we hire you?" is, "I know what to do next."

If you are having a meeting, research the attendees, create an agenda, and put together packets. If you have a project on the horizon, develop an outline, timeline, and budget. If your boss is stressed about the amount of work she has to get done, ask what you can do to help. Before you ask a dozen questions about a new initiative, do a little homework and try to figure things out on your own. It shows initiative and resourcefulness. Google your questions, look to other organizations doing similar work, get advice from a mentor, and be creative. It is much more impressive to work with an employee on a well-thought out proposal than it is to continually answer questions and walk them through every step of the process.

Anticipating needs and preparing for them allows you to maintain creativity and avoid boredom. Your ability to be the one who can plan a move ahead benefits the team and makes you invaluable. Don't ever let yourself get bored. There is always something to be doing because you can always get better. The author Charles Bukowski once said, "Only the boring get bored." Read, write, listen, learn, and grow into a more accomplished professional each day.

Rebel Without a Cause

Many of you, particularly those who are looking to get ahead in the workplace, are go-getters by nature. You got to where you are by being fearless and pushing boundaries. You want to be the best. These are great characteristics and will most likely serve you well. However, these personality traits can also be liabilities, and it's important to distinguish between being proactive and being a pain in the neck.

Based on your boss, it's typically okay to ask questions and suggest alternatives. A good boss wants to hear differing opinions and ideas from his or her staff. You are hired to do a job because you showcase expertise and skills that are needed by your organization. You should be an asset to your boss and a complement to your colleagues. You have a distinct voice, and you are paid to bring your unique abilities and perspective to the workplace.

It becomes a problem, however, when you are constantly or publicly disagreeing with your supervisor. If you cross the line into disrespectful territory, you will cause friction. If you notice that you are being poorly received, have a conversation with your boss and figure out the balance that makes you both comfortable in terms of how much feedback he or she expects from you.

Being the boss is difficult. You may not understand every decision she makes and that's usually because you don't have access to as much information as she does. It is typically wise to give your boss the benefit of the doubt. However, if you don't respect or agree with her on a regular basis, then you should find a different job. If you think your boss is making serious errors (particularly if veering into unethical territory) then you can elevate your concerns to the next level. Just be prepared to be rebuffed. Your boss is (theoretically) where she is because, she too, earned it. She probably has the respect of her superiors. When you are the boss, you will make the decisions and appreciate the employees who are an asset, and not a liability.

Remember the Power Differential

As an employee, you don't get to choose your boss, and in your career you will report to a variety of individuals. Some will be good supervisors, many will be mediocre, and a few will be poor. If you have a boss or supervisor with whom you work well, consider yourself lucky. You can learn a lot from your boss, and she or he might serve as a mentor for your career.

When you feel comfortable with your boss, or you have a lot in common such as age, hobbies, children, or mutual acquaintances, you may begin to think you are on equal footing or even that you are friends

It is important, though, to remember that the boss-employee relationship always contains a power differential. Your boss determines when your probationary period is over, what your assignments are, and approves your leave time and business expenses. Most importantly, your boss evaluates your performance and recommends raises and promotions.

You may be surprised by some observations your boss includes in your annual review. Perhaps you have expressed negative opinions about your company or its policies. Maybe you have cut corners somewhere or you have occasionally left early to miss the traffic. You thought being a little late with that one assignment or missing that big meeting was okay. You had no idea these would be negative factors on your evaluation, and your boss will always be the one who has the authority to make these assessments.

Maintaining professional boundaries in the workplace is a must, especially with your supervisor. You and your boss can be colleagues, can enjoy working together, may travel together for business purposes, and may have a similar work style or sense of humor, but don't ever forget who holds the power.

LIFE MATTERS

Benefit From Your Benefits

When looking for a first job, salary is generally the yardstick used for measuring the quality of the job. Oftentimes, a new employee doesn't pay much attention to other benefits even after they begin employment. Most young people know they should have health insurance, but may not ask about what portion the employee pays. They may know how many vacation days they get annually, but may not realize they have to accrue the time before they can use it. Sick time has a special purpose and shouldn't be misused. Life insurance may not seem essential when you are in your twenties, but it becomes critical if and when you have children.

Probably no benefit is less understood and more underutilized by young employees than retirement benefits. Retirement seems so far away that saving for it seems unnecessary when first starting out.

Few companies still have traditional (defined compensation) pension plans. Most now have defined contribution plans, usually in the form of 401k plans. Each year, the company generally sets aside a defined amount equal to a percentage of an employee's salary. Some employers also offer what is called a "match" (meaning they will match what the employee contributes to the plan). This is similar to additional salary and it will help you begin a lifelong savings plan. These are also important for young people because they often can take the money they contribute and the matching amount from their employer with them if they change jobs. Not participating in a match program is like leaving money—your money—on the table.

Be sure you understand and take advantage of all your benefits. Do your homework. Talk to colleagues, family members, and your benefits coordinator. You are serious about your salary. Be equally serious about your benefits.

Escape Route

When you were little, your parents probably discussed how to get out of your house in an emergency and probably taught you your address and how to call 911. At school you had to practice fire drills and classroom evacuations so you knew what to do in the event of a fire or tornado. When you learned to drive, your parents might have insisted you learn how to change a tire or attach new windshield wiper blades. You knew where the insurance card was and what information to collect if you were in an accident.

As we get to be adults, we seem to feel more secure, and less emphasis is placed on danger and emergency preparation. Yet terrorism and workplace violence have never been greater. It is important for your organization to have a disaster preparedness plan. Every employee should know what to do if they need to escape from the building or shelter in place. Don't just be familiar with the stairwell or fire extinguisher nearest your office. You may be in a meeting on the other side of the building when an emergency occurs.

You should know how to quickly contact building security or the police. Post emergency phone numbers prominently in case you are too frightened to recall them when needed. If your emergency contact information changes, be certain to alert Human Resources at your earliest convenience.

Being prepared shouldn't stop at the office exit. Employees who travel should be observant wherever they are. Pay attention to the flight attendant when she goes over emergency procedures. At your hotel, check the emergency procedures for your room and be sure you can find the nearest stairs. Some geographic areas are more prone to tornadoes, earthquakes, or blizzards, even volcanoes, and the safety instructions may be different for each.

It only takes a few minutes to be prepared, but the few minutes that you save during an emergency may mean the difference between life and death.

In Sickness and In Health

Not all employees who work fulltime get separate sick day benefits. Some companies simply don't offer them at all. So, if you are out sick, you don't get paid for the time you don't work. Other companies use a method called combined leave. You are given a certain number of days per year—maybe 20 or 30. You can use these days for vacation, illness, bereavement, or personal reasons. If you aren't sick that year, you can take more vacation days.

Most organizations, however, still offer traditional and separate sick leave. You generally accrue so many hours per month, and you can carry a certain amount over each year. This approach is meant to provide a safety net in case you do get sick or have an accident that prevents you from working. The accrued sick leave may also be used for women who take maternity leave or for the gap you might have to cover before receiving disability.

Like any savings account, you know the resource is there, and you may be tempted to use it. You may want to attend a weekend event that will be held out of town. If you call in sick on Friday and Monday, you could take that long weekend and save two vacation days for later.

Perhaps you have already used your two or three personal days. You need to get your car serviced, but you don't want to take a vacation day for such a routine chore. So, you call in sick again. While you are in the waiting area for your car, your boss walks in. It just so happens she is having her car serviced that day, too, and you are caught in a lie.

A similar situation can occur if you are taking a "mental health day" and think you can fit in the company gym in the middle of the afternoon which is usually a dead time. Or, you decide to see a movie or go to the mall. It's during the work day, so you should be safe. As you are leaving, you run into another employee or the head of Human Resources. Not only is it embarrassing, but it can be costly to your professional credibility.

Stories like these are common, as are stories of individuals being fired for abusing sick time or falsifying attendance records. The best practice is to learn to manage your time so that you don't run out of vacation and personal days, and you aren't tempted to misuse your sick day benefits. Your reputation is simply too important to risk.

Keep At It

We are inspired by athletes, artists, authors, and musicians who spend years honing their crafts. We are awed by people who overcome adversity to realize their dreams and goals. We watch wounded veterans learn to walk and function again. We cheer for survivors of illnesses when they rebound and become advocates for others.

We wonder how people like these maintain their passion and find the strength to reach new heights. What they have in common is perseverance. They may fail time after time. They may become discouraged and disappointed, but they don't stop trying. They don't give up.

Think about your personal goals. What are you working toward and what do you want to achieve this year, next year, this decade?

If your goal is to get a graduate degree, keep at it. It might take you longer than you expected or hoped, but, course by course, you eventually will arrive at the number of credits needed.

If you want to break into a certain field, keep trying. Develop a game plan and work at networking. Take risks. Try new things. Get extra training. Find a mentor.

If you want to be a CEO or if you want to build and run your own business, stay the course. There may be setbacks and uncertainty, but you can put them behind you and keep moving forward.

Nothing great was ever achieved without hard work, dedication, and, most importantly, perseverance.

Safe Haven

As you proceed through your career, you will face challenges, personally and professionally, that are extremely trying. Your relationships, family, health and mental health, and finances will need attention. Accidents, misunderstandings, and emergencies will happen. You will be discouraged, upset, and distraught. Life doesn't stop the moment you walk into your office.

In order to be successful at work, however, you do need to learn how to compartmentalize. If you are facing something really distressing, you should take the day off or leave the office. Know your organization's policies on bereavement leave and mental health services. Find out if they offer an employee assistance program (EAP). To the extent that you are comfortable, keep your boss apprised of major life events. You don't have to go into detail, but it can help her to understand and accommodate you. It may also be helpful to view work as a reprieve from these challenges. That may not always be possible, but you do have to find a way to function. Work can often keep you grounded and give you something positive and familiar to focus on when the rest of your world is chaotic.

If you need to access mental health services in order to deal with psychological or emotional challenges, do it. Take precautionary efforts with your health and support your own well-being. Taking control can help to offer stability. Spending every moment obsessing over situations beyond your control will only make them seem worse.

The Currency of Current Events

Some people, especially those in political jobs, are news junkies. They follow every election or bill introduced in the legislature. They always seem to know what is going on, and they may bore you with their constant political analysis.

Other individuals are sports fanatics. They know all the match-ups and statistics and who's ahead in the rankings. Their moods can rise and fall with the success of their favorite team.

Still others are enamored of celebrity. They follow entertainment news and can talk about who is dating whom or the latest fashion worn by the stars.

None of these areas may entice you, but having at least a working knowledge of them all is a good idea because it allows you to interact socially with coworkers and clients. You should know how the home team fared last night, or who was elected mayor. It doesn't hurt to know what movie won the award or what book is number one on the best seller list.

Keeping up with world events and with news especially relevant to your occupation is important, as both can have an impact on your job. There are many ways to stay current. You can get alerts on your phone or office computer. You can take a few minutes each day to scan an online newspaper, listen to a podcast, or watch news clips online. Subscribing to a trade magazine or relevant journals can keep you in the loop.

Being well-rounded is always an asset. Being able to participate in a conversation at a business dinner or being able to make small talk with clients before a meeting begins is critical. In the long run, you will find that it's well worth the effort to stay current.

The Power of "Yes" and the Strategic Use of "No"

When you accept your first job, the clock is ticking. You begin to build your professional reputation the second you step into the front door on your first day. Every email you send, interaction you have, and initiative you take comprises the foundation for the rest of your career. It's important to be known as someone who is dependable, trustworthy, and hardworking.

One of the best ways to do this is by being the employee who takes on new tasks and doesn't shy away from assignments. Not only does this help you consistently gain new skills and knowledge, but it also makes you a valuable asset to your organization. You don't want to be the "yes woman" in the sense that you never question things that don't seem right, you don't challenge established ways of thinking, or you find yourself a sycophant. However, you do want to be the person who seeks out new challenges, stays late when necessary, and comes up with new ideas and is willing to do the work necessary to bring those ideas to life. You must understand the power of "yes."

The challenge is that there are times when you should probably say "no." Young women are often tasked with errands and requests that are, in fact, below their pay grade and intelligence level. Cleaning up after a meeting or event, grabbing coffee for the group, or making copies are typical tasks people assume young women will and should do. We all do these things from time to time, but you don't want to be known as the go-to resource for mundane tasks. Sometimes you have to strategically use "no." This balance is delicate, but understanding it will serve you well if you learn how to utilize it early in your career.

100 Percent of Effort vs. 100 Percent of Time

You worked hard to secure your new position and you want to be successful. You are determined to do whatever it takes to stand out and get ahead. You are high energy and long hours don't scare you. As the months go by, though, it starts to feel like you are working longer and harder than your coworkers. Most of them leave at a reasonable time, and they seem to be enjoying social time or family life or heading off to the gym. Often, they ask you to check or finish something for them for the next day. You begin to feel like an assistant or a scapegoat instead of an equal. This is not what you expected or wanted.

Long hours at the office are not always seen as positively as might be expected. Some people may think that you are simply trying to impress the boss. Others may think that you have to stay late because you are incapable of getting your own work done during regular hours. Others may assume you have no family or social life and that you work late to fill your time. So, they avail themselves of your time.

If you find yourself in this position, think carefully about how you can alter it without being too abrupt or going overboard. Don't berate your coworkers. Don't whine. Don't feel sorry for yourself. Instead, start by slowly cutting back on your hours. Start staying late only if there is a true deadline and a team effort, or if your boss asks you to do something, or if the boss is going to be there. If you do need to finish an assignment of your own before a deadline, consider doing it at home.

Giving 100 percent effort on the job does not equate with giving 100 percent of your time. You can be a team player or a standout employee and still have a personal life.

Why Borrow Trouble?

When stressed and overloaded, many of us have a tendency to make ourselves more anxious by reverting to behaviors we thought we had outgrown. Perhaps we keep talking about how busy we are or use negative self-talk. Telling yourself and others that you can't possibly get everything done by the deadline simply amplifies the problem. Instead, try to tone down the panic and begin sending yourself a new message that you always manage to get done on time, and you will this time, too.

If you are really in a crunch, take a look at your list and see what can be omitted or put off. Be ruthless. Take a rain check on lunch with a friend, or see if someone else can cover an external meeting. Be selective. If exercise helps you stay calm, keep the gym on your to-do list, but cancel your manicure for the week.

Next, map out what you must accomplish and break it into components. Estimate the amount of time needed for each. Are there pieces you can delegate or can you ask a coworker to assist with one or two areas? Decide which is more important, trying for perfection or meeting the deadline? Are there corners you can cut that really won't make a difference? If so, now is the time to simplify.

Stop going over possible negative outcomes, and don't exaggerate the situation which can make things seem worse. Does your annual review actually depend on this one meeting? Will you be fired if things don't go as planned? Probably the answer to both is "no." Introduce some accuracy. You're no longer the little girl saying, "Everyone hates me," or the teenager shouting, "I have nothing to wear."

You're a professional with a track record for success in the workplace. When you move beyond old behaviors, your worry and anxiety will morph into motivation and action. Success won't be far behind.

Work Will Fill the Time

A work-life balance is a matter of perspective. Granted, many jobs are demanding. Some jobs require you to be on call, while others entail shift or weekend work. Due to advanced technology, you can now work from anywhere, and the boundary between work and leisure time is hard to maintain.

There are 168 hours in a week. Most fulltime jobs require your presence in the workplace for 40 hours. If you are lucky, you sleep 40 hours. Add 10 hours for commuting to and from work. That still leaves 78 hours each week for the life side of the equation. Even the weekend from 5 p.m. on Friday till 8 a.m. on Monday is 63 hours. After subtracting sleep time, you still have the equivalent of a whole work week available to you on the weekend.

So why does "free time" seem to be in such short supply? Part of it is due to those loose boundaries between working at work and working at home. Being disorganized is another time thief. Overscheduling activities, even enjoyable ones, can add to your stress level. Perfectionistic tendencies are a time killer. But perhaps the biggest culprit is your inability to say "no" to requests from others.

To get a better handle on how you spend your time, keep track of all your activities for an entire week. Evaluate what was important, what you could have eliminated, and what you can change for the following week. This exercise should help you determine how you can protect more time for yourself and your family.

We all get the same amount of time each week. Some people are masterful at using time effectively. Others squander hours and wonder where time went. You may not be able to control your schedule at the office, but you do control your personal time. Make sure time spent is really worth your time.

FOOD FOR THOUGHT

What's the Worst That Could Happen?

You finish your internship and you're interested in a fulltime position. You have been working hard and you can show your results, so you'd like a raise. You respect someone in your field, and you'd like them to be your mentor. A big secret to success is simple: ask. Ask for what you want. Ask for what you need. Ask for what you are worth.

When you are preparing to ask, always think, "What is the worst that could happen?" We have all been told "no." That's an opportunity to ask for constructive criticism so that you can enhance your skills and perform at the level that is required for professional growth. Your request should be reasonable, well-informed, and based in the reality of the situation. For instance, you probably are not going to get a raise if your organization is dealing with financial challenges. However, that is a good time to take on new roles and exhibit to your boss that you are willing to step in and help when times are tough. Learn more about budgeting and cash flow, or marketing and membership, and come up with potential solutions. You want to be known as someone who pulls her weight and is willing to be flexible and creative to help the organization. You do not want to be the office whiner who always thinks they are worth more but has done nothing to prove it.

If you are consistently told "no," it is either time to reevaluate the work that you are doing to determine how you can perform better, or reevaluate whether you should stay with your organization. Simply asking for what you want or need can lead to reduced educational debt, new positions, raises, promotions, and diverse experiences that contain important knowledge. Think about what you've potentially left on the table as a result of not asking for it. Momentary disappointment or even embarrassment is better than being left behind because you're not willing to ask for what you deserve.

Knowledge Is Possibility

The quote "Knowledge is power," is attributed to Sir Francis Bacon in 1587. The Latin translation is "scientia potentia est." "Potentia," or "power," also forms the root for the word "possibility."

In academic and scientific circles, knowledge building is a significant endeavor. In business circles, it is the application of knowledge that counts.

For example, your college degree indicates that you have certain knowledge about a subject area. It also indicates that you have the possibility of applying that knowledge in the workplace.

As you build your career, college degrees become less important than work experience. One shows your knowledge base. The other shows your knowledge application. While basic knowledge is important, current knowledge is critical. Change today is constant and fast paced. Keeping up with your field and with relevant business issues is a challenge, yet it is essential to success.

Begin by reading news lines, trade magazines, books, and blogs on a regular basis. Keep your certifications, credentials, and licenses current. Attend conferences and find time to network with colleagues both within and outside your specialty area. Then connect the dots so that you can stay focused on the bigger picture and the possibilities open to you.

Shifting Sands, Shifting Loyalties

A reorganization at the office can be unsettling for everyone. It may involve changes in reporting relationships, changes in job descriptions, different office locations, and a revised work plan. Reorganizations can be particularly difficult if they are a surprise, if staff don't know the reasoning behind them, and if they create a shift in workplace culture. Also, if downsizing is included, everyone grows uneasy. It's hard to watch coworkers be dismissed, and you may wonder why one person went and another stayed.

If you end up reporting to a new boss, there are several steps you must take. The first is to shift your loyalty to the new person. Get to know her and her management style, and support her both in public and in private conversations. Try not to compare her to your previous boss and don't discuss one boss with the other.

Different people require different levels of loyalty. For some bosses, loyalty is more important than competency. Loyalty may be one reason why a young go-getter is downsized, yet a more seasoned employee with mediocre skills is retained.

Shifting loyalty is not always easy. You might have worked well with your previous boss and liked her open door approach, her sense of humor, or her directness. Your new boss may have a completely different management style that feels rigid and formal. If this is the case, it will be up to you, not your boss, to adapt. Think of it as a new job or simply luck of the draw. You won't be in that position forever. Make the best of it and see what you can learn from a difficult situation.

Success and Self-Worth

We enter a new job with high hopes. The goal is to perform well and to get ahead, to be recognized and rewarded for our efforts. Progress, however, may be slow, and you may feel that success is eluding you. You may even begin to doubt the possibility of success or your own ability to move forward.

Self-doubt can call into question your self-worth. Feeling like a failure can sap your energy and depress both your mood and your work ethic. It can further undercut your chances of success.

Each of us has a definition of personal and professional success. Make sure yours is realistic, both in terms of time and outcome. For example, did you hope to be promoted in six months when a year is the norm at your workplace? Were you expecting a bonus or salary increase that far exceeded what you received? Was your evaluation less glowing than you had anticipated?

Each disappointment deserves an objective review on your part. Were your expectations grounded in corporate reality or were you a bit naïve? Did your performance fall short of what was needed? Most importantly, what can you learn from the situation that will help you in future endeavors?

Sometimes it is useful to privately chart or document small successes. Did a presentation go especially well? Were you invited to a high level meeting? Did you receive an email from a client thanking you for your assistance? These successes may prove useful when discussing a future evaluation with your supervisor. More importantly, a growing list of triumphs, even minor ones, may help offset doubts about ability or self-worth when faced with a disappointment in your job.

Professional success is based on many factors, only some of which you can control. Personal success, however, is entirely up to you.

Searching For Gold

Each of us has an idea about our "dream job" and career success. We envision meaningful work for which we are well-paid and recognized. Flexibility, autonomy, and security may figure in. Some want to be the boss; others want to be their own boss. Still others want to avoid management altogether and be free to create or perform.

A dream job can be a good goal. It can help keep you motivated and moving forward. It can encourage you to obtain further education or experience. Or it may inspire you to go in a different direction.

The idea of a dream job can also be a career detriment. Instead of inspiring you, it can make you restless and dissatisfied with your present position. You might feel you are deserving of more or that your road to the top shouldn't take you as long as it is. You may compare yourself to colleagues who have many more years of experience and dismiss how long they worked to get where they are.

If your desire for a dream job is interfering with your commitment to and success in your current position, do an objective evaluation of both your expectations and timeline. It might be helpful to research the career path of individuals in jobs such as the dream job you want. Better yet, talk with professional colleagues. Ask them how many "dream jobs" they have held in their careers and how they came about. You may be surprised to find that the idea of a dream job at the start of your career is a bit unrealistic. On the other hand, you may find some helpful hints about how to move forward in a more focused way.

Like Olympic athletes who compete for gold medals, dreams are essential. However, success depends on hard work and perseverance.

Fail Your Way to Success

Adults constantly warn children to "be careful." Every time you tried something new—riding a bicycle, driving a car, playing a sport—you received the same advice. As you got older and began to travel—to college, on vacation, or out of the country—the concern was always safety. Be careful.

Sometimes this message of caution seeps into other parts of our lives. We become so careful that we start avoiding risks in school, at work, and in relationships. The thinking is that, if you avoid risk, you will avoid failure.

We need to stop the mantra of caution and recognize the importance of both risk and failure. Progress is closely linked to risk taking. In fact, most great achievements begin with a risk. Risk can make us stretch our thinking, stretch our creativity, and stretch our performance.

In similar fashion, failure can make us grow. It forces us to take a hard look at what we could have done differently. It teaches us lessons about ourselves and our world. It spurs us on. It makes us better. As we become more adept at rebounding from our failures, we can use them as stepping stones to bigger and better things. To be successful in our careers, we have to move out of our comfort zones—our careful comfort zones—to uncharted territory.

Career Building Blocks

Once you have secured your job, you may feel you can forget about your résumé. That would be a mistake.

As you build your career, you should also be building a résumé that documents your professional work experience and your enhanced and growing skill set. At a minimum, review and update your résumé at least every six months. When you do, add any new job responsibilities or change in job title. In a separate file, keep a running list of professional presentations you deliver or any special training or certification you receive. You will find this useful if a new employment opportunity comes along or you may need it for your annual evaluation.

Pay attention to résumés that cross your desk. A great deal can be learned from reviewing the résumés of colleagues, external contractors, conference speakers, and up-and-coming workplace stars. Think about what impresses you in someone's résumé and what turns you off. Never copy or plagerize someone else's résumé, but good ideas about format and word usage are there for the taking.

Many professionals keep a web presence on sites such as Linkedin. If you do so, make certain you update that on a regular basis as well. While the format might be different, the content describing your work experience should be conistent with your written résumé.

You might want to have both a shorter functional résumé and a longer chronological one. If you are in an academic environment, you will want to explore the components of a curriculum vita.

It is also helpful to keep a current one paragraph biography that can be quickly submitted, if requested, for a meeting participant list as well as a 50 word paragraph that can be used to introduce you. If you work in an organization that writes and submits grants, you should develop a uniform biosketch like ones that are generally required in grant proposals.

Nothing shouts "lazy" more than using an outdated bio or résumé. Get in the habit of keeping your professional information organized and quickly accessible so that you never miss an opportunity to advance in the workplace or in your career.

Values Conflicts

Employees are not always in sync with workplace goals and decisions. Depending on the issue, our personal experiences and viewpoints may differ to a greater or lesser degree from our colleagues or even from our boss. Discrepancies in views can create both personal and public tension. Learning to manage this difference of opinion is critical to your success on the job.

Let's assume you did the research necessary to vet your employer and its public policies before you accepted the position. If so, you shouldn't have been too surprised once you began employment. Some things, however, are harder to discover before you are in the office. These subtleties include acceptance of religious practices, the treatment of women, and the openness to diversity, especially diversity of opinion.

There are some practices that are never acceptable: violating laws, ethics or civil rights, mistreatment of staff, sexual harassment, and threats of violence, to name only a few.

Other practices have less apparent consequences but may be upsetting to you nonetheless. You may be surprised to find that the organization leans toward one political party, and you are firmly in the other camp. You may have differences of opinion about environmental issues, reproductive rights, income inequality, and issues of war and peace. How do you manage these issues?

The first thing is to keep your personal opinions personal. You don't have much to gain by being open about your personal viewpoint if you know it conflicts with the prevailing view at work. If your employer sponsors certain causes or events about which you disagree, you can quietly turn down an optional invitation to a gala or luncheon. If it is an organizational event, however, you may have more difficulty not participating. That event would be a good time to have a private exchange with your supervisor expressing your concern and asking for a substitute assignment.

If you do volunteer work for a cause or community organization, keep those activities separate from the workplace. Don't try to recruit members or support. Don't use any organizational resources or direct correspondence to your work email. Outside of work, you have the right to participate in any issues important to you, but there is little to be gained by criticizing your employer in a public forum.

Sometimes the differences between your beliefs and your work culture are simply too great to bridge. At that point, it is wise to start looking for a position more consistent with the values you hold.

Job Lock

The average worker no longer stays with one organization for life. Goals, interests, and opportunities can change rapidly, and it's now the norm to move from position to position, and even from profession to profession, as you follow your personal career path.

We have been taught that it's not good to job hop, that we need to stay in each position long enough to learn the ropes and have some successes. Ideally, our résumés should show forward movement both in skills learned and responsibility level achieved.

Just like you can leave a job too soon, you can also stay in a job too long. There is no hard and fast rule. Sometimes it depends on your chosen profession. It takes many years to achieve tenure at a university or to make partner in a law firm. Medical residencies and research fellowships vary in length based on specialty and funding. Artists and performers may struggle for years, working in temporary jobs until their big break happens.

Those employed in businesses or agencies or government positions may have more opportunity for advancement by changing jobs to climb the career ladder. Sometimes, though, they get locked into a job. Maybe employment in their area is sluggish. Maybe they need the benefits provided, or they are trying to finish a degree, or they are simply afraid to take the risk. Sometimes inertia takes over. They are ready for bigger things, but finding a new job seems too hard, even overwhelming.

There are many employees who simply love the jobs they have and don't want to change, and that's okay. People who love their work and who are satisfied with their salary and benefits are lucky.

Other times, though, employees feel they can't leave because their agency or their clientele needs them too much. This frequently occurs in social service agencies and the helping professions. This feeling of being indispensable is a red flag and is often a clue that someone is verging on burnout. We also forget that we might be able to have a greater impact for our clients if we move into a job where we can affect policy and improve service delivery in the community.

Each of us needs to decide how long we stay in each job. However, if you would like to leave, but feel you can't, take a hard look at your situation. Remember that you are the one driving your career. Get some career counseling. Talk to a mentor. Make some plans. Get some training. Take some risks. Don't accept being locked in. The longer you stay, the harder it will be to get out, and your career may stall out shortly after you cross the starting line.

All's Well That Ends Well

Many years ago, Shakespeare memorialized that statement in a play by the same name. Today we take that phrase to mean that despite difficulties and disappointments, a situation will be okay if it turns out well in the end.

Sometimes leaving a job does not turn out well. You may be so relieved to get out from under your old job, and so excited about starting a new job, that you decide to stop working as hard. You may be tempted to cut corners or begin using your sick time as vacation time, or do a half-hearted job on your last project assignment. Don't let that happen.

Just as you have only one chance to make a first impression, you have only one chance to leave well. When you are gone, your final attitude and behavior are what your supervisor or boss will remember most clearly. You never know when you will need a reference—some jobs require them from all of your previous employers. You also may underestimate how small your field is and how many people know each other in both your old and new organizations.

Be as professional when you are leaving as you were when you first took the job. Complete all assignments. Give at least the required amount of notice. Make the transition as easy as possible for your replacement. Show up and show up on time. Be cordial to everyone. Don't say negative things about the workplace or your colleagues, even though they may be the reason you are leaving. Don't gloat about your new job. Adhere to all office policies and make sure you leave with your integrity intact and your conscience clean.

You worked hard to make a good first impression. Work just as hard to make a good last one.

ABOUT
THE AUTHORS

Elizabeth (Betsy) Clark, PhD, is the President and Co-Founder of Start Smart Career Center. She is an experienced CEO and national leader who has held executive positions in health care, nonprofit organizations, and academia. A lifelong advocate for women's rights and economic equality, she serves on numerous boards of directors of cause-related or professional associations, and is a champion for increasing the number of women in board leadership positions. Her current emphasis is on mentoring young women for workplace success and career advancement.

With degrees in social work, public health, and medical sociology, Betsy is a recognized expert, author, and speaker on the topics of cancer, hope, loss and grief. She has traveled extensively and has a particular interest in hospice and palliative care in underserved countries. She and her husband love the mountains and live in the Catskill Mountain region of New York. They have three children and four grandchildren.

Elizabeth F. Hoffler, MSW, is the Executive Director and Co-Founder of Start Smart Career Center. She is a social worker, public policy, and advocacy professional who has advanced quickly from entry level jobs to positions of leadership and management in national nonprofit organizations. She attributes much of her success to having strong women mentors who pushed her to take advantage of every opportunity and accomplish her professional goals no matter the obstacles.

In addition to her work in nonprofits, Elizabeth is also a PhD student and is focusing her studies on underserved and vulnerable populations, and finding innovative, policy-oriented solutions to some of society's most pressing problems. Elizabeth lives outside of Washington, DC with her husband and two pugs, Bubbles and Bonkers.